FIVE CENTURIES OF

WOMEN & GARDENS

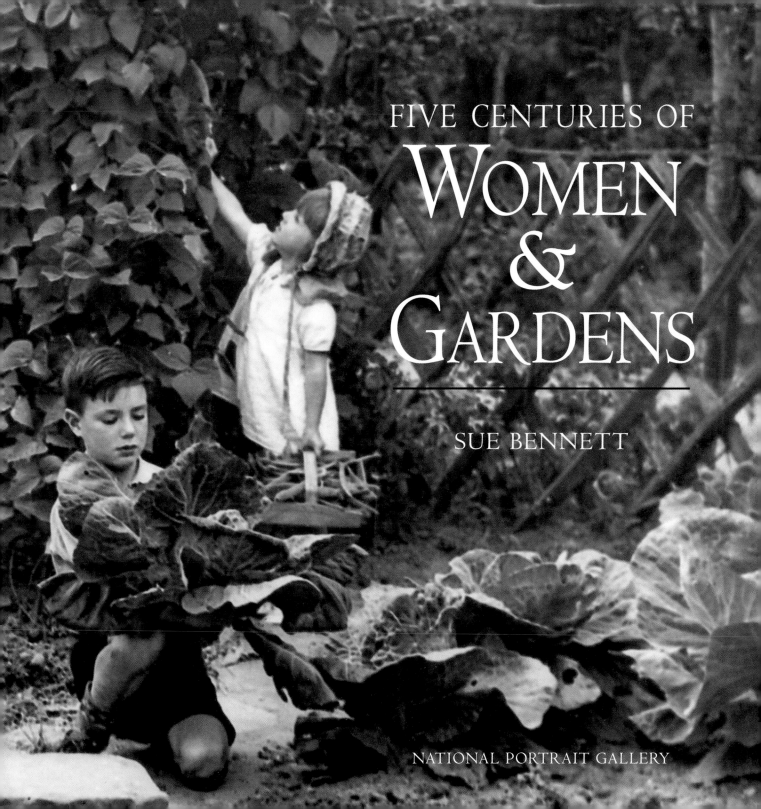

FIVE CENTURIES OF
WOMEN
& GARDENS

SUE BENNETT

NATIONAL PORTRAIT GALLERY

Published in Great Britain by National Portrait Gallery Publications, National Portrait Gallery,
St Martin's Place, London WC2H 0HE

Published in connection with an exhibition sponsored by FLORIS

For a complete catalogue of current publications, please write to the address above, or
visit our website on http://www.npg.org.uk/pubs

ISBN 1 85514 288 0
A catalogue record for this book is available from the British Library.

Publishing Manager: Jacky Colliss Harvey
Editor: Susie Foster
Designer: Karen Stafford
Production: Ruth Müller-Wirth

Printed by Conti Tipocolor, Italy

FRONT COVER: *The Capel Family*, c.1640. NPG 4759 (detail)
BACK COVER: Marie Studholme, 1903. Museum of Garden History
FRONTISPIECE: *Dig for Victory*. Imperial War Museum (detail)

For Clive Burgess and Clare Gittings

❧ CONTENTS ❧

Preface

When I told friends in Central and Eastern Europe that I was writing a book on women and gardens, they looked at me with amazement. Writing a book on women must seem strange in societies where school history is dominated by grand narratives, mostly about men. Writing a book on the history of gardens must seem even more bizarre but a history of women and gardens was almost beyond belief. Could such a study be serious history?

A passion for gardening and garden history is not confined to these islands, but both are quintessentially British pursuits. Other nations garden, but the British have made gardening into an art form now deeply embedded in the national psyche. But why write a history of women and gardens?

After all, women's relationship with gardens is not, in many instances, so different to that of men. Women have designed and cultivated gardens; cooked, preserved and arranged their produce; drawn and written about gardens and plants; and flirted, intrigued and made love in gardens. Men have done the same. But men and women have perceived their relationships to gardens in different ways. For much of the period of time covered by this book, prevailing attitudes to gender barred women from owning property or land in their own right and made them subservient to men. This book explores women's roles as gardeners, patrons, designers, educators of women gardeners, plant collectors, writers, campaigners, artists and illustrators against such a background.

There is a wealth of material on garden history and a number of other studies on women and gardens. I, however, have written the book that I wanted to find when I first became interested in this topic and found that despite the many books on garden history and gardening, no one had related the history of women and gardens to that of women's emancipation in its broadest sense. What I hope I have produced is an entertaining sweep through the topic, setting the stories of significant women gardeners against developments in garden history and women's role in society. It is in that sense an original work, but in order to see I have had to stand on the shoulders of many much more experienced historians of gardening and of women than myself. I make no secret of my immense indebtedness to the work of others. In a book without footnotes it is difficult to credit other writers and researchers, but I have tried to make my indebtedness clear in the bibliography and by textual references. I would like particularly to acknowledge my dependence on the work of Sir Roy Strong on Renaissance and royal gardens, and on Dawn

MacLeod's, Helen Penn's and Deborah Kellaway's work on women and gardens, on Adrian Tinniswood's work on garden visiting and Dea Birkett's on Marianne North and women travellers. Heartfelt thanks are also due to Jane Brown who read the manuscript of this book for me and whose many works on garden history are all classics of the genre. Almost all the plant lists in this book derive from her studies, and without her this book could not have been written. I hope she will accept my emulation as the sincerest form of respect. Any mistakes are, however, my own.

My thanks are also due to Graeme Curry for his help on Marianne North; to Imogen Magnus for information on Daisy, Countess of Warwick; to Karen Hearn for material on Lucy, Countess of Bedford; to Margaret Ellis for help with literary and theological references; to Tony Berry for information on Sunnycroft and for showing me the garden; to Professor Eric Evans for his advice on social history; to Canon John Inge for commenting on the Introduction; to Sylvia Bennett for her inspiration, and to Nigel Nicolson. I owe a particular debt to Oliver Garnett for his unfailing courtesy in answering enquiries and for reading a draft of the text. I am also indebted to Anne Laurence for her advice, friendship and for comments on the text.

I am grateful to the staff of the Lindley Library; the *Country Life* Picture Library; the National Trust Photographic Library, and to other Trust staff. I am grateful to my publisher and editor at the National Portrait Gallery, Jacky Colliss Harvey and Susie Foster, for their help, and to the staff in the Gallery's Exhibitions, Design, and the PR and Development departments. My family, friends and colleagues also deserve my thanks for enduring my enforced seclusion and obsessive interest in women and gardens without complaint.

This book would not, however, have been written without the support of two people to whom I am deeply indebted. Clive Burgess has been a tower of strength, reading the text, searching for lost commas, improving my prose and providing support through so many 'lonely teatimes of the soul' that I now no longer dare count them. Clare Gittings, Education Officer at the National Portrait Gallery, and I dreamt up the exhibition that this book supports over lunch in the depths of the crypt of St Martin-in-the-Fields. Clare masterminded the exhibition and suggested that I write this book, and I am grateful to her for failing to tell me what the task involved and then supporting me through the process by feeding me with information, providing treats and making me laugh. This book is, therefore, dedicated to both Clive and Clare in gratitude for their friendship.

Introduction: Escape to Eden

In the beginning was a garden, a fertile, peaceful place, a haven of earthly delight. And we were banished. The sense of loss, whether of self, of childhood, or of past perfection, haunts our imaginations. And so over the centuries we have sought to recreate this place of pleasure – an enclosed world in which we can express our desire for perfection. Gardens reveal our inner selves. What we create is inevitably subject to change, growth and decay. But there is sometimes a vestige remaining, an image of our vision of perfection, preserved for the future and revealing our relationship with the natural world, with society and with ourselves.

The image of the garden as paradise has always been strong in Christian iconography. The word 'paradise' comes from Persia where it meant an enclosed garden. It is, perhaps, a difficult symbol for women. The Bible contains two myths about the creation of man and woman. In the first (Genesis 1:27 and following), man and woman are created together, presenting an image of equality. In the second (Genesis 2:18–25), Eve, created from Adam's rib, is an afterthought, a subservient 'helpmate' for Adam. Genesis portrays Eve as the temptress, her disobedience responsible for the couple's expulsion from Paradise, and for the beginning of 'all our woe' (Milton, *Paradise Lost*).

Eve's counterpart, the Virgin Mary, mother of Christ and the bearer of redemption, is an image of responsiveness, wholeness, fecundity and transformation, and undoes Eve's disobedience. Christ, the new Adam, is mistaken by Mary Magdalene for a gardener after the Resurrection, thus ushering in not a return to the pre-lapsarian world of innocence, but a new Eden of moral responsibility and forgiveness. The Virgin Mary can, however, also be seen as an image of passivity and docility. Adam can be interpreted as the archetype of male control of the environment, and a dominating, patriarchal figure.

For almost two millennia, belief in the Creation, Fall and Redemption, as mediated by the teachings of the Church, profoundly influenced the relationship of men and women to the environment. This tended to stress the dominant role of men and to place

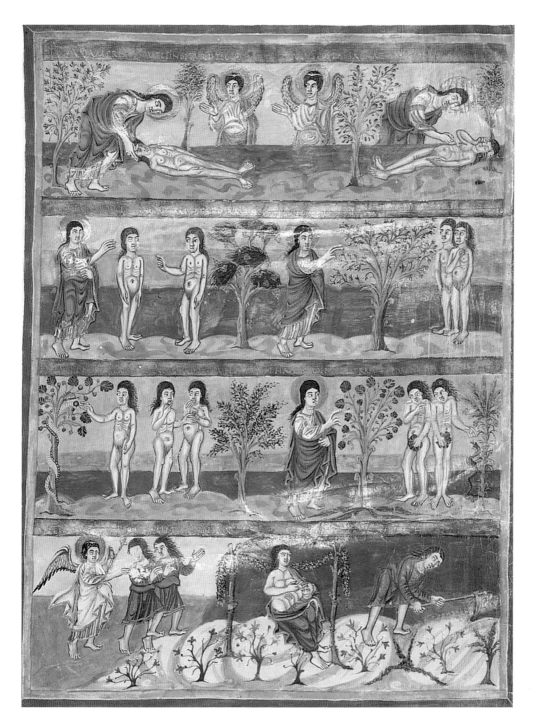

The Creation and Fall of Man
The Moutier-Grandval Bible, Genesis
The British Library (ADD 10546 f5v)
Tours, 9th century

This 'picture strip' shows the creation of Eve from Adam's rib, a story that for centuries was used to authenticate the subservient status of women. After the expulsion from Eden, Adam's inheritance was work, while Eve's lot was the pain of childbirth. Here she sits under a garland suckling her baby and surrounded by a flowery meadow.

a value on docility and passivity in women. In medieval art, the closed world of the garden was often used as a symbol of heaven. Immured behind a hedge or wall, the Virgin is portrayed sitting on a turf bank, surrounded by flowers rich in symbolic meanings. This is the image of the 'hortus conclusus', the enclosed garden, inspired by the description of the beloved in the *Song of Solomon* from the Bible:

> A garden inclosed is my sister, my spouse;
> A spring shut up, a fountain sealed.
> Thy plants are an orchard of pomegranates, with pleasant fruits;
> Camphire with spikenard,
> Spikenard and saffron;
> Calamus and cinnamon, with all trees of frankincense;
> Myrrh and aloes, with all the chief spices;
> A fountain of gardens,
> A well of living waters
> And streams from Lebanon.

The image of the woman in the secluded garden is redolent of the restricted life which many women led, set apart from the worlds of government, the law and commerce.

Medieval gardens were small-scale enclosures in what was often seen as a threatening wilderness. In England such views persisted until the late sixteenth and early seventeenth centuries, when the last vestiges of wasteland were tamed. Visions of paradise still, however, dominated the minds of garden designers. For example, the seventeenth-century vogue for botanical gardens can be seen as an attempt to perceive the mind of God through reason. The Botanic Garden in Oxford, founded in 1621, was a visual representation of the Divine Order, with the four quarters of the garden, a living encyclopaedia of God's creation, containing plants from the four continents of the known world, laid out in strict hierarchical order. But in the end the pursuit of rational order undermined the search for Eden. Man, as he unlocked the secrets of the natural world, came to believe that he, not God, was at the end of the evolutionary trail, and this shift in perception was mirrored by changes in the status of woman.

Throughout the eighteenth, nineteenth and twentieth centuries, women struggled to gain control of their lives and to assert their right to equality in the home and outside it. The stories of the women in this book show how through five centuries, gardens functioned as physical and spiritual arenas in which individual women strove to assert control, define their identity, struggle with sexual feelings and escape or embrace the world.

Gardens exist in the mind and in reality. Our perceptions of gardens weave together ideas and sensitivities: what we think and what we feel. Throughout the history of gardening, this balance between action and contemplation has shifted constantly. In a largely post-Christian England, the image of the garden still has strong spiritual and therapeutic overtones. Carl Gustav Jung saw the garden as central to the concept of wholeness, an image strongly related to the mother archetype and linked with fertility and fruitfulness. For him, the garden was the enclosed space in which transformation could occur, and the physic garden, with its healing plants, functioned as an image of emotional growth and the alchemy of change. For many women the garden, both as a real place and as a metaphor, continues to fulfil this role. Despite progress towards equality, Eden still haunts us. The stories of other women chart the route in a quest for paradise that still remains a potent symbol, inspiring new generations of women to transform themselves and their world.

The Annunciation
Fra Filippo Lippi, late 1450s?
Tempera on wood, 685 x 1520mm (27 x 59⅞")
National Gallery, London

In medieval sermons the Virgin was referred to as the hortus conclusus. *This was a poetic reference both to paradise and to Mary's virginity. In Lippi's painting, Mary sits in a loggia facing an enclosed garden. In front of her, on a low wall, is an urn containing a Madonna lily, the symbol of purity. The Angel Gabriel carries a spray of the same flower as he kneels before her. The reflection of his pose by the Virgin is suggestive of mutual self-giving rather than domination. At the top of the picture, the hand of God emerges from a cloud.*

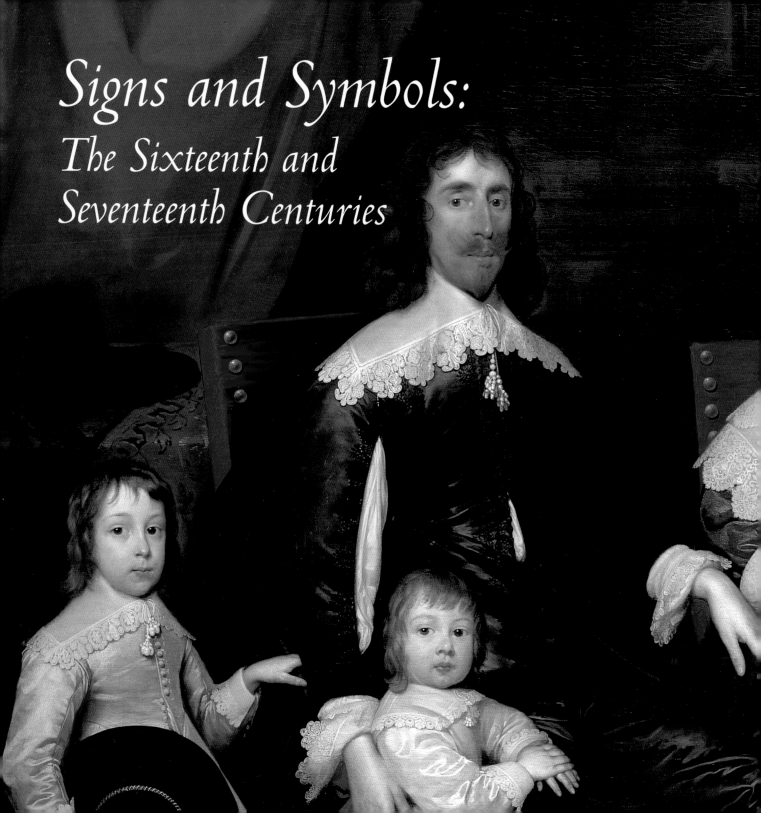

Signs and Symbols:
The Sixteenth and Seventeenth Centuries

Introduction

Changes in the design of sixteenth- and seventeenth-century gardens marked out man's increasing physical and intellectual conquest of nature. During these two centuries the small, intimate medieval garden was supplanted by symmetrical gardens of increasing size and complexity. Elaborate geometrical patterns defined the main spaces of the garden while avenues of trees marched across the landscape as outward signs of man's superiority and dominance, and natural forces were harnessed to drive mechanical devices and automata.

Women, however, had little chance to conquer anything; almost all were subject to the will of fathers, brothers, husbands or male guardians. The demands of home and family further constrained their horizons. Gardens were a part of this world, as sources of food and medicines, but they were also arenas in which women could make some of the few independent decisions open to them. Very few could command the earth be shaped as they desired; becoming patrons of garden designers and collecting and classifying rare plants were possible only for women of independent wealth and power.

The changing nature of gardens

Medieval gardens, often portrayed in art as walled or hedged enclosures, were small-scale oases of order in what was seen as a wild and uncontrolled environment. Late medieval garden features included patterns of clipped, low-growing hedges, known as knots, and arbours of intertwined roses or evergreens. During the Tudor period knots became more elaborate, with galleries and terraces providing platforms from which to view their designs. Privy or private gardens were positioned under the windows of the principal apartments of a house so that the knot designs could be seen by those within to best effect. Beyond such privy gardens more public spaces developed, again containing symmetrical designs of knots and leading to walks and *allées* made from pleached trees shaped to form shady tunnels. These were spaces for flirtation and intrigue, as depicted by Shakespeare in *Much Ado About Nothing* (1598–9), where Beatrice is lured into 'the pleached bower, where honeysuckles, ripened by the sun, forbid the sun to enter' (III.i), while Hero and Ursula walk up and down the alley talking of Benedict.

During the early seventeenth century more monumental and formal parterres replaced the knot. The most elaborate was the *parterre de broderie*, or embroidered parterre. This was a symmetrical geometric pattern in clipped box, often of great complexity. Increasingly, English garden design was influenced by fashions brought from Italy and France and by the work of continental garden designers such as Salomon de Caus (1576–1630). De Caus, an engineer, inventor, gardener, and producer of masques, was employed by such important patrons as Anne of Denmark (1574–1619; see page 26) wife of James VI of Scotland and I of England, and by their son Henry, Prince of Wales (1594–1612). De Caus's gardens, which featured giants, grottoes, speaking statues and water-powered organs, depended upon a rediscovered understanding of air pressure and hydraulics. But the mechanical figures and statues found in them were not just physical demonstrations of scientific principles; they were also allegories of myths, intended to provoke contemplation.

Royal marriages brought further foreign fashions in their wake. Henrietta Maria (1609–69; see page 28), wife of Charles I, was responsible for the visits of the French designer André Mollet to England. Exile during and after the Civil War brought the royal family into contact with the great gardens of France and the Netherlands, while the arrival of William III and his wife Mary in 1688 popularised Dutch ideas of gardening and horticulture. By the end of the seventeenth century, cultivation had transformed the wild. Nature appeared tamed, and house and garden were integrated into a unified landscape of symmetry and geometry.

Women's worlds

Although, as has been said, the position of a woman in sixteenth- and seventeenth-century England was determined by her gender and by her husband's or her father's social class, upper-class women might evade some of these restrictions. Apart from sovereign queens, they were debarred from formal political processes, excluded from aspects of the legal system and enjoyed only limited access to economic control of their lives. The only women who had free control of property were widows, unmarried heiresses and the few women whose families had insisted upon marriage contracts that restricted the husband's access to his wife's property.

In the literature of the period, women were identified as an error of creation, an imperfect version of man. Eve's intellectual and moral weakness was thought to be the primary cause of the Fall, and consequently women were considered naturally insubordinate, hypocritical, lustful and garrulous. These inclinations were controlled through the promulgation of an image of the perfect woman – obedient, chaste, pious, subservient, and preferably married.

Debarred from the political and legal world, women exercised more independence in the domestic sphere. Here family life, religion and friendship helped to create a system of communal support, providing some protection from the dominant and sometimes predatory male.

Food and medicine

Gardening, and its attendant activities, was an occupation in which all women could participate, regardless of social status. Distilling home-made medicines and making preserves were part of women's work, and for many women, growing vegetables and herbs was not only an important economic activity but essential for survival. In grander gardens though, the gardeners were often men, with women being employed only as weeders, just as in noble households, the cooks were men, and women were responsible only for the basic preparation and serving of food.

The kitchen and herb gardens were thus women's responsibility, and a number of books were published to help women in their tasks. The Protestant emphasis on Bible reading had ensured upper- and middle-class women were taught the rudiments of reading. In 1557 the agricultural writer and poet Thomas Tusser published *One Hundred Pointes of Good Husbandrie* and in 1573, this became *Five Hundred Pointes of Good Husbandrie*, covering farming, household matters, storage of food, gardening and the distillation of remedies.

GOOD huswives provides, ere an sicknes doo come,
of sundrie good things in hir house to have some.
Good Aqua composita, Vineger tart,
Rose water and treakle, to comfort the hart.

(Thomas Tusser, *Five Hundred Pointes of Good Husbandrie*)

William Lawson's *Country Housewife's Garden* (1617) was the first gardening book for women. Exchanging herbs, recipes, medicines and cordials helped women to cement their social relationships. John Goddard, a London physician, wrote in 1670 that 'worthy ladies and gentlewomen of quality, do employ themselves in making confections, and medicines both internal and external.' Tending plants, producing food and caring for the sick offered women a defined role, as well as the ability to make independent choices.

The Onion (detail)
One of the thirty-two octagonal canvas-work panels displayed in the Drawing Room Passage at Hardwick Hall Each Octagon is 355mm (14″) The National Trust

Signs and symbols

Flowers had been used as religious motifs in medieval paintings: the lily signified the Annunciation, four-petalled flowers, such as stocks, symbolised the Crucifixion, while violets and columbines were associated with melancholy and death. Daisies, roses and strawberries were all linked to the Virgin. With the Reformation the complex iconography of the medieval church was transmuted into more secular propaganda, as in the imagery used and encouraged by Elizabeth I.

Elizabeth I

Clever, manipulative and parsimonious, Elizabeth I (1533–1603) ruled England through a shrewd mixture of diplomacy, caprice, sudden anger and simulated petulance, controlling her nobles by playing games of coquetry, preferment and financial reward in return for loyalty, service and adulation. Even as the 'Virgin Queen', the game of courtship remained both a diversion and a political strategy. Her nobles competed for her favour by building sumptuous houses in which she might be entertained on her progresses round England, creating allegorical gardens and planning elaborate, open-air spectacles for her amusement.

In 1591 Edward Seymour, 2nd Earl of Hertford (1539?–1621), organised the most complex of all the outdoor entertainments of Elizabeth's reign. He created, at his house at Elvetham, Hampshire, a vast crescent-shaped lake, with three islands: one had trees on it, representing ships' masts, a second had a fort 'built' by Neptune, and a third had a huge mount, 12 metres in diameter and 6 metres high (40 x 20'). A spiral-shaped privet hedge rose to the top of the mount. Elizabeth, as the moon goddess (she was frequently depicted as Diana the virgin huntress, with her symbol, the crescent moon), ruled over the lake and the spectacular mock naval battle, which was put on for her pleasure, symbolising the defeat of the Spanish Armada by the English navy in 1588.

In May 1591 William Cecil, 1st Baron Burghley (1520–98), Elizabeth's Lord Treasurer, entertained her at Theobalds, his house in Hertfordshire. One of the welcoming speeches was spoken by a gardener and described a garden created by Burghley's son, Robert Cecil, 1st Earl of Salisbury (1563–1612), to demonstrate his family's loyalty to the Queen. This garden had at its heart an arbour of eglantine roses – another of the Queen's symbols. In one of the knots surrounding the arbour, the Queen was symbolically worshipped by the Twelve Virtues, represented by roses, by the Three Graces, symbolised by pansies, and by the Nine Muses, depicted as several other types of flowers. The world was thus literally at Elizabeth's feet.

Elizabeth as Diana

Elizabeth I (1533–1603) (detail)
Attributed to Nicholas Hilliard, c.1575
Oil on panel, 787 x 610mm (31 x 24")
National Portrait Gallery, London (NPG 190)

This detail, taken from the portrait of Elizabeth reproduced opposite, depicts her holding an eglantine rose, one of her symbols.

In the horticultural symbolism of the period, images of the Queen and her prosperous realm, of Astraea, the just virgin, of May-time and the birth of a golden age, all combine to create the mythical figure of Gloriana. Such images were mirrored in contemporary art and literature. The Queen's symbols, the red and white Tudor rose, and the single five-petalled eglantine rose, often appear in her portraits. The poet Edmund Spenser in *The Shepheardes Calender* (1579) associated her with the flowers of spring. On the head of the Virgin Queen he describes a

> Cremosin [crimson] coronet
> With Damaske roses and Daffadillies set:
> Bayleaves betweene,
> And primroses greene
> Embelish the sweete Violet.
>
> (*The Shepheardes Calender*, 1579, 'Aprill')

The symbols of the Virgin Queen employ many of the same motifs that had belonged to the Virgin Mary, whose month was May and amongst whose flowers were the lily and the rose. Bess of Hardwick used horticultural imagery to demonstrate her loyalty to the crown.

Elizabeth I (1533–1603)
Attributed to Nicholas Hilliard, c.1575
Oil on panel, 787 x 610mm (31 x 24")
National Portrait Gallery, London (NPG 190)

In this portrait Elizabeth wears as a jewel the
pheonix, the mythical bird of which there is only
ever one, thus symbolising her unique position as
Queen. The pheonix was also used as a symbol
of Elizabeth in her gardens.

Bess of Hardwick (Elizabeth Talbot, Countess of Shrewsbury; 1527–1608)

Hardwick Hall still dominates the Derbyshire landscape, fixing in stone the character of Elizabeth Talbot, Countess of Shrewsbury, its proud and imperious builder, whose initials surmount the parapets of her home and who is known to history simply as 'Bess of Hardwick'. Born into a gentry family, Bess was a serial widow, who rose through successive marriages to be one of the richest women in England. Her fourth, and most spectacular marriage, was to George Talbot, 6th Earl of Shrewsbury (1522–90), but after its collapse (caused in part by their tense joint custody of Mary, Queen of Scots), Bess retreated from Chatsworth, the home of her second husband, Sir William Cavendish (1505?–57), to Hardwick, the place of her birth. Here she improved and embellished the Old Hall (now ruined) and then, in 1590, started to lay foundations for a new, larger and even grander house.

Little detailed evidence survives for the layout of the gardens that once surrounded the new house, although the walls and courtyard are original. Hardwick surmounted a lightly wooded landscape, designed to provide cover for deer and game, and this setting, and the symbolism associated with it, was introduced into the house. The imagery of the natural world was used both to demonstrate Bess's loyalty to the crown, and as an exercise in self-aggrandisement by Bess herself – one of

Exterior view of Hardwick Hall (looking through an archway, along a pathway to the front of the building)
The National Trust

'Hardwick Hall, more glass than wall' was built between 1590 and 1597 by the architect Robert Smythson (c.1535–1614). Bess of Hardwick, Robert's patron and Hardwick's owner, proudly decorated its skyline with her initials ES (Elizabeth Shrewsbury).

her personal symbols was also the eglantine rose, which had been the emblem of Sir William Cavendish, and which is seen on her coat of arms, supported by stags. The Old Hall had contained a forest chamber, and the plasterwork in the High Great Chamber of the New Hall depicts a hunt, at the centre of which is Elizabeth, again shown as the goddess Diana, surrounded by lilies, foxgloves and gillyflowers – all symbols of virginity. But although they are the focal point of the picture, the Queen and her court are passive. Equipped with bows and arrows, they await the arrival of the animals rather than actively pursuing them. The male hunters, further round the frieze, put on their crampons and climb the hills to seek the deer. On the far wall the unicorn, another reference to virginity, shelters in a forest.

Bess's interest in the natural world is also evident in the needlework found throughout the house. Women often spent their time sewing and embroidering and at Hardwick a collection of octagonal canvas-work panels depicts plants and herbs derived from continental books of botanical illustration. Each plant was ascribed a text. For the onion this was 'many may talk but few are wise' (see pages 18 and 24).

Elizabeth Talbot, Countess of Shrewsbury (1527–1608)
Unknown artist, probably 17th century after a portrait of c.1590
Oil on canvas, 988 x 787mm (38⅞ x 31″)
National Portrait Gallery, London (NPG 203)

Patronage, friendship and fashion

Gardens allowed owners to show off not only their wealth but also their knowledge of fashionable design, poetry, the Bible and classical mythology. Although the main patrons and designers of the period were men, some women also helped disseminate new garden design ideas. Anne of Denmark's patronage of Salomon de Caus has already been mentioned. Isaac de Caus (*c*.1576–1626), the nephew of Salomon, worked for women patrons including Lucy, Countess of Bedford (1581–1627; see page 27), at Moor Park, Hertfordshire and Bedford House in London, and possibly for Lady Anne Clifford (1590–1676), at Wilton House, Wiltshire. At Heidelberg in Germany De Caus built, in 1613, an elaborate garden for Elizabeth, Queen of Bohemia (1596–1662), daughter of James VI of Scotland and I of England and Anne of Denmark, and wife of the Elector Palatine. This included terraces, knots, parterres, fountains, grottoes, an aviary, a water parterre and even a speaking statue.

Six of the thirty-two octagonal canvas-work panels displayed in the Drawing Room Passage at Hardwick Hall
Each octagon is 355mm (14″)
The National Trust

These linen octagons, finely worked in silk and wool, depict plants and flowers from a botanical book by Pietro Andrea Mattioli. The inscriptions round the edges were taken from the Adages of Erasmus. The octagons were probably intended to be sewn onto curtains or hangings.

Metaphor and allusion

Real gardens provided settings for spectacular displays such as water tournaments or *fêtes champêtres*; imaginary ones, painted on stage sets, became backdrops for court masques. The elements of garden design, such as statues, grottoes and watercourses, carried messages which, like the symbolism of court masques, were designed to be contemplated and absorbed. Thus the real and the imaginary merged in a complex raft of metaphor and allusion. Only those within the relevant circle of power and patronage or who had been educated in classical mythology were able to identify and interpret this synthesis of real and imaginary worlds.

Anne of Denmark's garden at Somerset House (started 1609) was designed for Anne by Salomon de Caus to symbolise her role as Queen. The central terrace was entered through a loggia on the south front of the house, while a vast Parnassus fountain dominated the east garden, with Apollo and the Muses forming its centrepiece. Round the sides of the fountain reclined four river gods, representing the principal rivers of Great Britain, each resting on an urn which spouted water. Sir Roy Strong has suggested that the fountain is a celebration of Anne as Tethys, queen of nymphs and rivers and wife to Neptune, which had been the subject of a court masque in 1610.

Lucy, Countess of Bedford's garden at her house in Twickenham Park, was designed to foster contemplation and was laid out in a series of circles within a square, three of birch and two of lime, with an outer circle of fruit trees. Flights of steps at each of the corners led up to vantage-points, from which the visitor viewed the design, a representation of the pre-Copernican universe, in which the sun and the planets revolve around the Earth. Radiating outwards from the Earth, the visitor saw Luna, Mercury and Venus (birch circles), Sol and Mars (lime circles), Jove (the fruit tree circle) and Saturn beyond. The imagery of light and stars used in this garden has been linked with that of the writers and artists whom Lucy patronised.

The garden at Wilton, Wiltshire, which as Sir Roy Strong has explained was built in the brief period (*c.*1630–35) when Philip Herbert, 4th Earl of Pembroke (1584–1650) was living in harmony with his wife, the redoubtable Lady Anne Clifford, was designed around the theme of love and chastity. Lady Anne was a noted patron and builder in her own right. She rebuilt castles on her Cumbrian estates, founded almshouses and erected monuments. Isaac de Caus was employed by Pembroke as the garden's designer. The statues in the parterre were of famous women: Venus cradling Cupid, Diana, Susanna and Cleopatra. The gardens on either side of the central groves of trees symbolised ideals of behaviour appropriate to men and women. As in the court masques of the time, the female virtues are those of chaste love, while men were to espouse the heroic virtues of the loyal knight.

Anne of Denmark (1574–1619) and Lucy, Countess of Bedford (1581–1627)

Anne of Denmark (1574–1619)
Marcus Gheeraerts the Younger, c.1611–14
Oil on canvas, 2210 x 1310mm (87 x 51½")
By kind permission of the Marquess of Tavistock and the Trustees of the Bedford Estate

Anne of Denmark had married James I in 1589, when he was King James VI of Scotland. Although she bore James six children, her husband's homosexuality, court favourites and drinking precluded a warm and happy marriage. James did not in any case think very highly of women. When it was suggested that his daughter Elizabeth of Bohemia should learn Latin the King forbade it on the grounds that 'to make women learned and foxes tame had the same effect: to make them more cunning'.

Anne was the sister of Christian IV of Denmark, creator of one of the most cultured courts in Europe. She had an excellent eye for artistic talent and sophisticated tastes in poetry, court entertainment and garden design – qualities which were inherited by her children and which she herself employed in the costly

Plan of the gardens of Somerset House
Robert Smythson, c.1609
Sepia, pen, 280 x 265mm (11 x 10½")
RIBA Library

This drawing shows the parterres and the Parnassus fountain in the east garden.

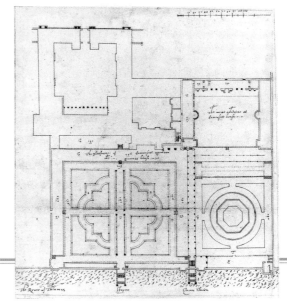

diversions with which she sought to keep herself amused. Anne had the gardens at Greenwich and Somerset House redesigned and commissioned Inigo Jones (1573–1652) to build five gateways for the garden at Oatlands in Surrey. One of her closest friends was Lucy, Countess of Bedford. Lucy possibly commissioned Marcus Gheeraerts the Younger to paint the portrait of Anne (left). The background of the painting may serve to show us what the west garden at Somerset House might have looked like.

The sole heiress of Sir John Harington of Exton, Lucy was rich, cultivated, beautiful and extravagant. In 1594, aged thirteen, she had married Lord Edward Russell, 3rd Earl of Bedford (d.1627). Her husband retreated from court life after a fall from his horse, but Lucy remained gregarious as well as culturally ambitious.

Lucy took part in a number of spectacular court masques, some of which Anne helped to direct. Their shared interests in gardening and drama bound them together, as did their friendships with a circle of poets and artists that included Inigo Jones, John Donne (1572–1631) and Ben Jonson (1573–1637).

Lucy's garden at Twickenham Park was an exercise in symbolism. She parted with Twickenham in 1617, when James I granted her the estate of Moor Park in Hertfordshire. Between 1617 and her death in 1627 she poured money into the design of her new garden, as well as collecting plants with which to embellish it. Isaac de Caus's design probably included a terrace, a large parterre divided into quarters with gravelled walks and adorned with eight statues, summer-houses, two cloisters, a grotto with shell and rock work, fountains, water works, a wilderness full of fruit trees, and a further wild garden with more fountains. Lucy lavished considerable time and energy on Moor Park, requesting plants and advice from her friends and 'adding som trifles of pleasure to that place I am so much in love with …'

Possibly Lucy, Countess of Bedford (1581–1627)
Unknown artist, c.1603
Oil on canvas, 1914 x 1138mm (75⅜ x 44¾")
National Portrait Gallery, London (NPG 5688)

Rest and repose

As well as providing backdrops for spectacles, gardens were planned to include walks, wildernesses and groves designed to provoke meditation. This was, in part, a response to the sixteenth- and seventeenth-century interest in melancholy, one of the four humours which influenced behaviour. Melancholy, although cold and dry, was seen as a characteristic of intellectual genius. It was thus an ambivalent state and the walks and groves were designed both to stimulate the intellect and to stave off the depression and black bile with which melancholy was often associated.

The gardens of Elizabeth, Duchess of Lauderdale at Ham spanned both these aspects of melancholy, as scenes of artistic and intellectual endeavour, and in the end a place of lonely solitude.

A view of the Cherry Garden at Ham House, Surrey
The National Trust

Cherry trees, which gave the Cherry Garden its name, were probably planted against the walls of the garden. In 1975, the National Trust used John Slezer and Jan Wyck's drawings of c.1671–2 to restore the Cherry Garden. Compartments surrounded by dwarf box hedges are planted alternately with santolina and lavender. Berceaux (vaulted trellises) of pleached hornbeam surround the garden in the middle of which is a statue of Bacchus, the only free-standing sculpture to survive from the Lauderdales' garden.

Family traditions

One of the most significant gardening dynasties of this period was the Capel family. Johnson's portrait of the family, painted in 1640, shows Arthur Capel, 1st Baron Capel (1604–49), and his wife together with their five children. The picture mirrors a portrait of Charles I and his family, and is a visual demonstration of Arthur's devotion to his king – loyal to the last, Arthur was executed shortly after Charles in 1649.

Arthur's wife, Elizabeth, was the daughter of Sir Charles Morrison, a well-known gardener, and the painting shows in the background the family's garden at Hadham Hall, Essex. The garden has a formal, geometrical design, embellished with fountains and a terrace on which one can just make out pots containing tulips, then both fashionable and expensive.

The children inherited their parents' love of gardening. Arthur Capel, 1st Earl of Essex (1631–83), the eldest son, created a garden at Cassiobury, Essex. The youngest son, Henry Capel, 2nd Baron Capel (1638–96), who is shown sitting on his mother's lap, owned a garden at Kew where he built two greenhouses – one for oranges, the other for myrtles. Elizabeth (1633–78), who is presenting a rose to her baby brother, married Lord Herbert, 2nd Earl of Carnarvon, became Countess of Carnarvon, and took up flower painting. One of her paintings survives in the Royal Collection and Lely's portrait (reproduced on page 37)) of her with her sister Mary shows her holding one of her own works. Mary, the eldest daughter, became a noted gardener and a plant collector.

The Capel Family
Cornelius Johnson, c.1640
Oil on canvas, 1600 x 2591mm
(63 x 102")
National Portrait Gallery, London (NPG 4759)

Mary, Duchess of Beaufort (1630–1715)

Virtuous, devout and artistic, Mary Capel was a patron of garden design and a friend of the famous naturalist Sir Hans Sloane. She married Henry Somerset, 1st Duke of Beaufort (1629–1700), owner of Badminton in Gloucestershire, as her second husband in 1657, and together they rebuilt the house and laid out impressive gardens for which Mary collected plants.

Mary specialised in exotics and tender plants, which she nurtured in her conservatory, built in the 1690s, and in what she called her infirmary. The plants came from all over the world, in particular from Virginia and the Cape of Good Hope. Stephen Switzer extolled her in his *The Nobleman, Gentleman, and Gard'ners Recreation*, published in 1715.

What progress she made in exotics, and how
much of her time she virtuously and busily
employed in the garden is easily observable
from the thousands of those foreign plants (by
her as it was made familiar to this clime) there
regimented together, and kept in wonderful
deal of health, order and decency, if they are
now the same as seven or eight years ago, when
I had the happiness of seeing them with some
others. Besides her servants assured us,
excepting the times of her devotions, at which
she was a constant attendant, gardening took
up two thirds of her time.

She was also mentioned as having been
a generous procurer of plants from overseas in
the *Catalogue of Trees and Shrubs, both Exotic and
Domestic, which are propogated for sale in the Gardens near
London*, published in 1703 by the Society of
Gardeners.

In 1703, when she was again a widow,
Mary commissioned a record of her collection,
with pictures of flowers and butterflies mounted
on parchment. The first volume was the work of
a Dutch artist called Everhard Kick or Kik, who
worked at Badminton from 1703–5. The second
was by Daniel Frankcom, an under-footman with
a talent for drawing, who was trained by Kik on
the instruction of the Duchess. The flowers
illustrated include nerines, pelargoniums, guava
and hibiscus, although a few common flowers,
such as roses, pinks, gillyflowers, pansies and
violets, are also recorded.

Rationality and subservience

At the start of the Tudor period, wild men and women were still thought to lurk in the untamed woods. Gradually, however, the forest was forced into retreat, the fens drained; heaths ploughed up and waste places brought into cultivation. Attitudes to the environment began to change: reason and science, rather than mythology, governed man's relation to his world, and by the early eighteenth century landscape gardening and horticulture were semi-scientific pursuits.

In the woman's domain, little had changed. Upper-class women were not quite the passive, iconic figures who sit or walk in the gardens of illustrated medieval manuscripts – seventeenth-century paintings of women portray real individuals, however idealised. If in a garden, this is a world to which they invite the viewer, not one in which they are immured.

But women were nonetheless still regarded as irrational and lesser beings. They were excluded from formal political and economic structures, and their own communal and domestic world, linked by ties of family and friendship, was often conservative, inculcating in each new generation the virtues of marriage, docility and subservience. From the woman's point of view, the scientific revolution of the seventeenth century and the growth of rationalism had still not had that much impact on women's self-awareness or on men's attitudes towards women.

A View of Hampton Court
Leonard Knyff, c.1702
Oil on canvas, 1531 x 2163mm (60¼ x 85")
The Royal Collection © 2000, Her Majesty Queen Elizabeth II

This painting shows the gardens shortly before William's death in 1702. The semi-circular Fountain Garden lay beneath the east front and contained parterres of turf cut into patterns outlined by box hedges. To the north were the kitchen gardens and the wilderness, which contained the maze. Along the south façade were a series of small gardens, including Queen Mary's flower gardens as well as her hothouses and orangery.

Allusion and Illusion:
The Eighteenth Century

and Nicolas Poussin, all of whom had drawn on a common set of classical allusions. The fashion for foreign travel and the Grand Tour enabled nobility and gentry to see the ruined temples of Italy for themselves, as well as to buy pictures and statues as mementoes. Back home, they could use the statues to recreate their journey and their vision of an idyllic past. Having identified themselves as men of taste and refinement, they could then invite their friends and neighbours to appraise their work.

As Tinniswood shows, the eighteenth century saw the rise of garden visiting as a popular and fashionable pastime. Owners began to open their estates on pre-set days to meet demand; and by the end of the century there were even tearooms for the weary. Respectable visitors, well supplied with guidebooks and maps, followed prescribed walks along winding paths, encountering carefully contrived surprises – grottoes, temples and statues – all placed to provoke both contemplation and emotional response.

Visitors prepared themselves for the tour. Guided by the writings of William Gilpin (1724–1804), Richard Payne Knight (1750–1824) and Sir Uvedale Price (1747–1829), they learnt to value the picturesque elements in the landscape: its roughness, grandeur and composition. Some took a Claude glass on their travels to heighten their sensitivities and to change mere nature into the sublime.

Study of a man sketching using a Claude glass
Thomas Gainsborough, c.1750–55
Graphite, 184 x 138mm (7¼ x 5½")
The British Museum, London

The Claude glass, in fact a plano-convex mirror about 10cm (4″) in diameter, accentuated the foreground of a vista while the background disappeared in a romantic haze of blue. The viewer moved the glass so that he or she delineated a miniaturised view of the most affecting part of the landscape, thus transforming the English countryside into the Claudian ideal. The distinction between image and reality, picture and place, was blurred. One truly was in a landscape of illusion.

Despite the fact that these new landscape gardens were cheaper to build and maintain than the parterres and geometric designs of the previous century, still only women of great wealth could afford to commission such work. Elizabeth Montagu of Sandleford Priory, Berkshire, a widowed friend of the talented amateur Mary Delany, whom we will encounter later (see page 64), was exceptional, commissioning Capability Brown for what she saw as her 'paltry plans'.

> I … make a very paltry figure to him as employer. He is
> narrowly circumscribed, both in space and expense; but he
> really gives the poor widow and her paltry plans as great
> attention as he could bestow on an unlimited commission and
> an unbounded space.

Queen Caroline

Caroline Wilhelmina of Brandenburg-Ansbach (1683–1737)
After Sir Godfrey Kneller, 1716
Oil on canvas, 975 x 619mm (38⅜ x 24⅜")
National Portrait Gallery, London (NPG 529)

Although Caroline remained resolutely German, she appreciated the need to present herself as British. This influenced the decoration in her garden buildings at Richmond Lodge, which included statues, waxworks and marble busts of British worthies and philosophers. Her menagerie, including tigers, was a more exotic touch.

Queen Caroline (1683–1737), wife of George II (1683–1760), had both the money and position to act independently. Her garden at Richmond in Surrey, as Sir Roy Strong has shown, was designed to assert the legitimacy of the Hanoverian succession and to confirm her family's essential Britishness. Since both Caroline and her husband were German, and their claim to the throne rested on her father-in-law's Protestantism rather than his place in the direct line of descent, this was a delicate but important task.

Charming, bawdy and flirtatious, Caroline of Ansbach was adopted at the age of twelve by Sophie Charlotte, the Electress of Brandenburg. Caroline soon absorbed the intellectual interests of her foster-mother's court, apparently enjoying conversations with the philosopher Gottfried Leibniz, as well as sharing the Electress's love of gardening. Married in 1705 to the heir to the Elector of Hanover, the future George II, Caroline quickly discovered that her husband did not share her carefully cultivated interests. He hated intellectual pursuits and was scornful of her interest in gardens. Nevertheless, despite his infidelity, he remained devoted to his wife, who was well able to use her charm and manipulative powers to dominate him.

Gardening on the scale Caroline had in mind required significant amounts of money as well as land. Unfortunately, in the early years of her marriage, Caroline had insufficient access to both. George II and his father were locked in a mutual hatred of each other. Even when her father-in-law became King of England in 1714 and the whole family came to England, the animosity between father and son meant that the future George II was barred from the royal palaces, and kept on a meagre allowance. Not until 1727, when George I died, were funds available. Caroline then used her charm to beguile the Prime Minister, the worldly and cynical Robert Walpole, to persuade Parliament to grant her an annual allowance of £100,000 – an amazing amount, even for a queen. (Although the gift may have to be a ruined classical temple, surmounted by a bell turret. Inside, however, all was order: a bookcase, daybeds, and marble busts of scientists, philosophers and theologians including Dr Samuel Clarke, William Wollaston, Isaac Newton, John Locke and Robert Boyle. The philosophical message the observer was meant to infer was perhaps that the discoveries of science demonstrated the order of divine creation. Nature, rather than the formal garden, became the new image of Eden.

On Caroline's death the garden at Richmond was unfinished, and Caroline's debts amounted to £20,000 – a result, in part, of her extravagance as a gardener. Although conceived as a work of propaganda, Richmond also became a place of escape. As the poet Richard West (1716–42) perceived in his *Monody on the Death of Queen Caroline*:

> Within the Muses' bower
> She oft was wont to lose the vacant hour,
> Or underneath the sapiet grot reclin'd,
> Her soul to contemplation she resigned,
> And for a while laid down
> The painful envied burthen of a crown …

Plan of the House, Gardens, Park & Hermitage of their Majesty's at Richmond and the Prince of Wales's at Kew
John Rocque, 1736
The Royal Botanic Gardens, Kew

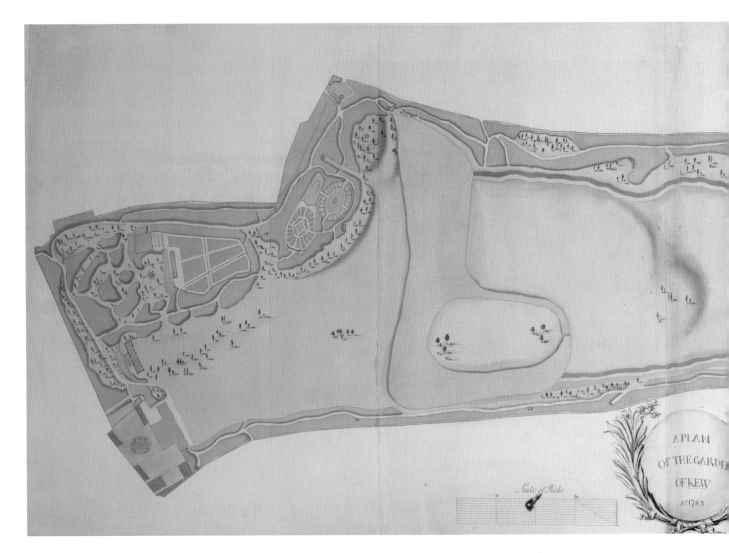

A PLAN
OF THE GARDE[N]
OF KEW
A:1763

Scale of Rods

A question of fashion

One essential for the fashionable garden was the possession of either a grotto or a hermitage, preferably with a live hermit (though it was hoped one who did not go on strike as the hermit at Painshill did). William Wrighte's *Grotesque Architecture*, published in 1767, provided the prospective owner with illustrations of a range of hermitages in a variety of styles. The wrong choice could be risky – Mary Delany for one had strong views on grotto design and criticised Lady Walpole's grotto severely: 'Grotto I will not call it. The

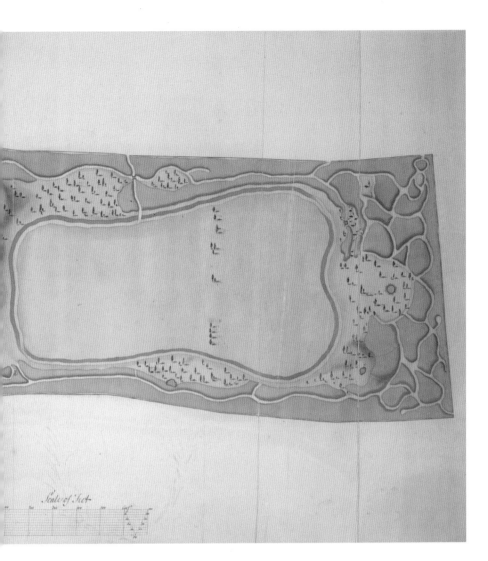

Plan of Princess Augusta's Garden at Kew, 1763
(Maps, K.Top.XL46.m.)
The British Library

regularity is abominable; besides all the coral is painted, mine shall not be made after that model.' (Quoted in Naomi Miller, *Heavenly Caves: Reflections on the Garden Grotto*, 1982.)

Embellishing the bare walls of a grotto was a suitable project for women; and by far the most fashionable way to do so was by using shells. This combined popular fascination with far-distant places with the skills of classification and decoration. As the writer Stella Tillyard has stated, the grotto shows that eighteenth-century rationality and women's alleged sensibility were thus blended; order and sentiment mingled together and transformed nature into a work of art.

The Grotto at Goodwood

The elaborate grotto built at Goodwood House in Sussex by Sarah, Duchess of Richmond (d.1751) and her eldest daughters Caroline (1723–74) and Emily (1731–1814) was begun in 1739, and completed seven years later. Built high up on the South Downs, with sweeping views towards Chichester Cathedral and the sea beyond, it used local flint and fossils on the exterior walls to give them a rude and rugged natural look, but inside was a different world. Thousands of shells, many brought from overseas and transformed into cornucopias of fruit or woven into swags, ribbons and bows, created a shimmering effect. Mirrors caught the light and reflected it over the pink, yellow and blue-grey shells. The floor was made from black marble and hundreds of horses' teeth. Unfortunately, we do not know how much of the work the women did. They may simply have chosen the design, selected the shells and supervised the work. But the result no doubt provided an ideal spot for an afternoon excursion.

LEFT
The restored ceiling of the shell grotto, Goodwood House, West Sussex
Tim Imrie-Tait, Country Life, *25 September 1997*
Country Life *Picture Library*

RIGHT
Interior of the shell grotto, Goodwood House, West Sussex
Tim Imrie-Tait, Country Life, *25 September 1997*
Country Life *Picture Library*

The initials of Charles Lennox, 2nd Duke of Richmond and his wife, Sarah, Duchess of Richmond, appear in the capitals of the piers that support the broad arch, alongside the initials of his eldest daughters: 'CF' for Caroline Fox and 'EK' for Emily Kildare. Jeremy Musson's article in Country Life *(25 September 1997) suggests that the work was carried out, or at least completed, between the marriages of the two daughters, in 1744 and 1747 respectively, and the death of the Duke in 1750.*

Patrick Delany's garden in Ireland accorded perfectly with Mary's tastes. She described it in a letter to her sister in July 1744:

These fields are planted in a *wild way, forest-trees and with bushes*, that look so naturally you would not imagine it a work of art … a very good kitchen-garden and two fruit-gardens which … will afford us sufficient quantity of every thing we can want of that kind. There are several prettinesses I can't explain to you – little wild walks, private seats, and lovely prospects. One seat I am particularly fond of in a nut-grove, and the beggar's hut which is a seat in a rock … is placed at the end of a cunning wild path, the brook … entertains you with a purling rill.

Mary encapsulated her interest in botany and gardening in her embroideries. The chair covers at Delville were decorated with embroidered plants. The high point was her court dress, a dazzling display of 200 different flowers, embroidered on an overskirt of black silk. The underskirt glowed with more flowers: winter jasmine, hawthorn berries, sweet peas, love-in-the-mist, lily of the valley, forget-me-not, anemone, tulips, convolvulus, bluebells and irises, all worked in long and short stitch.

At the age of sixty-nine as a widow, Mary was invited by her friend Lady Margaret Cavendish, the Duchess of Portland, to stay with her at her house at Bulstrode, near Gerrards Cross in Buckinghamshire. She became intimate with the Duchess's wide circle of friends – botanists, explorers, politicians, gardeners, artists, and even members of the royal family. Visitors to the house included Sir Joseph Banks, the botanist who had accompanied James Cook on his first voyage to the Pacific, and George Dionysius Ehret, a botanical artist. These new friends enhanced her knowledge and appreciation of plants and in 1772, led her into a new pastime of making flower collages.

Noticing by chance the similarity between a geranium and a red piece of paper, Mary cut out the paper into the shape of the flower, and then used more paper to create the leaves and stalk. This was the first of nearly one thousand botanically exact plant collages which she made over the next ten years. Many were copies of plants from Bulstrode; others were of plants from Kew, then in the care of Sir Joseph Banks, or from the Chelsea Physic Garden. The collages were mounted on black paper, pasted on the back of which were botanical notes that used the Linnaean sexual system of classification. Although she worked rapidly, Mary could cut with such dexterity that the intricacies of stamens and stigmata were all captured in the detail of collages.

Through the Duchess, Mary met George III and Queen Charlotte. Their common interest in gardens and botany led to a lasting friendship, so much so that when the

Rosa Spinosissima, *Burnet Rose [Rosa pimpinellifolia]*
Mary Delany
Flower paper mosaic
The British Museum, London

Queen Charlotte's Cottage at Kew
Built c.1770
The Royal Botanic Gardens, Kew

This rustic cottage, built, according to the London
Magazine *of 1774, to a design of her own, was
Charlotte's one addition to her garden at Kew.
Originally a single storey building, it was used as a
picturesque shelter for the royal family. Charlotte's only
real contribution was probably to the interior decoration.
On the upper floor is a picnic room, decorated by her
third daughter, Elizabeth, as well as a kitchen and a
waiting room.*

Charlotte was supposedly named for her. The Bird-of-paradise Flower, *Strelitzia reginae*, introduced into Kew in 1773, also honours her name.

Women's relationship to many aspects of eighteenth-century life was tangential. They were, for example, political hostesses rather than politicians. Much of middle- and upper-class women's influence was confined to the domestic sphere, as access to the more public worlds was restrained by convention as well as by their economic dependence. Men created landscapes; in the accepted order of things, women walked through the park, embellished the grottoes and classified the plants. But impressions of stability were illusory. Beyond the smooth surface of immaculate lawns, the forces of the industrial revolution were already evident.

The Picnic Room, Queen Charlotte's Cottage, at the Royal Botanic Gardens, Kew
Crown copyright: Historic Royal Palaces

Princess Elizabeth painted these brilliant blue ipomoea and scarlet nasturtiums, entwined round wooden poles, probably around 1805.

Mary Moser (1744–1819) and Frogmore House

Mary Moser was the daughter of a Swiss painter in enamels. Highly talented, at fifteen she won the silver medal from the Royal Society of Arts for a 'Polite Arts' competition, with a watercolour and gouache study of flowers that today still hangs in the Society's rooms.

The Academicians of the Royal Academy, 1771–72
John Sanders after John Zoffany, 1773
Watercolour, 188 x 270mm (7⅜ x 10⅝")
National Portrait Gallery, London (NPG 1437)

Mary Moser is the portrait on the far right.

Contemporaries record Mary as being 'so near-sighted that her nose, when she was painting, was within an inch of the canvas.' Nonetheless she was to become both the most sought-after and possibly the most expensive flower-painter of her day – her work decorating the pavilion at Frogmore was reputed to have cost £900 – perhaps the equivalent of £2.25 million in today's money.

Mary Moser's designs at Frogmore are highly patriotic and feature the symbols of the three kingdoms (the oak leaf and rose for England; the thistle for Scotland; the harp for Ireland) as part of the overall scheme. The source of many of the specimen flowers was Queen Charlotte's own flower garden and her prized greenhouse.

John Sanders' study (1733), after John Zoffany's *The Academicians of the Royal Academy, 1771–72*, includes the figure of Mary Moser, but only as a portrait hanging on the wall of the life-room of the Academy, where the study is set. Beside her portrait hangs that of Angelica Kauffman, another major artist of the period. The women occupy a prominent position behind the figure of the President of the Academy, but are being represented rather than actually present. While this may have been due to Zoffany's reluctance to endanger their reputations by depicting them in the life-room (from which women were excluded), it does aptly symbolise the position of women within society.

Flowerpiece
Mary Moser
Oil on canvas, 635 x 530mm
Royal Academy of Arts, London

This picture shows spring flowers, including daffodils and tulips. With its companion piece, of summer flowers, it was presented to the Royal Academy by Mary Moser herself. The paintings were not botanical illustrations, a genre in which she also worked, but aesthetic compositions.

Victorian Values:
The Nineteenth Century

Villa gardens could range in size from half an acre to three. Although commercial nurseries and seed catalogues offered a great deal of choice, garden style was in fact limited by convention. The up-and-coming might own a shrubbery, a specimen such as a monkey-puzzle tree and a lawn. A conservatory, a few fashionable flowers such as chrysanthemums and dahlias, plus some roses and a fruit and vegetable garden completed the picture. Once established, the garden could be used for croquet parties (from the 1860s) or lawn tennis (from the 1870s).

Park Town, built in 1855 in then rural North Oxford, is a good example of a small development in this period. The main terraces were built around a central garden planted with shrubs and trees, where dancing bears, performing dogs, German bands, Punch and Judy shows and organ grinders provided entertainment. The less expensive terraced houses had small back gardens; the more exclusive villas on the outskirts of the estate were advertised as having both front and back. Fashion-conscious buyers bought shrubs from Gees, a nursery conveniently situated in the neighbouring Banbury Road.

When the University began allowing dons to marry, Victorian Gothic villas set back from the road replaced Park Town houses as the most sought-after residences. They looked solid and respectable but their shrubberies provided good hiding-places for thieves from the nearby low-class district of Jericho. 'Scarcely a day passes without someone losing bedded-in plants, roses or some favourite potted flower,' complained a writer in the *Oxford Chronicle and Bucks, Berks Gazette*, 1876.

The rich

The old aristocracy inherited land; the new rich, grown wealthy on the proceeds of the industrial revolution and commercial speculation, bought land and built houses in the fashionable baronial Gothic style. To the owners, these vast piles, with their great halls, servants' wings, turrets and stained glass embodied the country virtues of hospitable good cheer as well as moral and religious endeavour. Victorian society could be as moralistic, if not more so, as any of the social orders that had preceded it, and a failure to observe its rules of decorum might result in a social exclusion similar to that suffered by Lady Luxborough in the previous century.

Lady Dorothy Nevill (1826–1913)
Private View of the Old Masters
Exhibition, Royal Academy, 1888 *(detail)*

Private View of the Old Masters
Exhibition, Royal Academy, 1888
Henry Jamyn Brooks, 1889
Oil on canvas, 1524 x 4064mm (60 x 160")
National Portrait Gallery, London (NPG 1833)

blue elevated spiritual qualities and green suggested hope. Women could even wear their messages, and their positioning too could add shades of meaning. Flowers in the hair meant caution, but flowers in the cleavage remembrance or friendship.

Working in the flower garden was even for middle-class women within the bounds of propriety. Jane Loudon (1807–58; see page 98), contemporary doyenne of gardening ladies, said:

> Whatever doubts may be entertained as to the practicality of a lady attending to the culture of culinary vegetables and fruit trees, none can exist regarding her management of the flower garden. That is pre-eminently a woman's kind of garden labour; only, indeed, to give an interest in its effects.
>
> (*Gardening for Ladies*, 1840)

Jane Loudon also did the flowers for her own home in Porchester Terrace. Instead of the formal style then fashionable, she created natural-looking flower arrangements and placed carefully selected pot plants around the house.

Flower displays in a grand house usually had to be imposing, luxuriant and costly. Elaborately dressed dining tables offered an opportunity to show off either prize specimens from the flower garden and the conservatory or fruit from the hothouse. Potted palms were displayed in their spacious halls. The middle classes took up the trend and in less wealthy homes a 'Wardian Case' (a glass container shaped like a small greenhouse) on the parlour table enabled them to show off a few specimen ferns. For middle-class dining, Mrs Beeton (1836–65; author of *Mrs Beeton's Book of Household Management*) recommended two to four bowls of flowers for a dinner party of six to twelve guests. These contained arrangements using only one or two colours and were surrounded by draped asparagus fern. The table must have been a trap for the socially unskilled for it also held napkins, cruet sets, bon-bon bowls, cutlery and candlesticks. Was there room for the plates?

Gardening for Ladies

Frontispiece of Gardening for Ladies
Jane Loudon (1840)

Gardening for Ladies, published in 1840, was Jane Loudon's greatest work. This is a practical book, full of clear instructions and based on her own quest for knowledge. Diffident as ever, Jane saw her amateur status as a qualification for authorship.

> I write this because I think books intended for professional gardeners are seldom suited to the needs of amateurs … Although it may appear presumptuous of me to teach an art of which for three-quarters of my life I was entirely ignorant, it is in fact that very circumstance which is one of my chief qualifications for the task … Having been a full-grown pupil myself, I know the wants of others; and having never been satisfied without grasping the reason for everything that had to be done, I am able to interpret these reasons to others.

> *(Gardening for Ladies, 1840)*

girl who has recently married and gone to live in the countryside. Jane instructs Annie on how to deal with a difficult gardener, on the importance of occupying her time in keeping bees and goldfish, on boating and skating and gardening. In Annie's garden, she recommends that gloomy trees are removed and replaced by formal beds full of sweet-scented roses, petunias, calceolarias, pelargoniums and mimulus. Phlox, double rocket and auricula are then added, and Jane suggests violets, heliotrope and mignonette for fragrance.

Other works followed but so did the bills. In 1850 Jane started editing a new journal, *The Ladies Companion at Home and Abroad*, aimed at serious-minded women. But although initially a success, sales declined, and Jane was replaced as editor by a man. She never recovered from the disappointment.

Paradise beyond the garden

Women travellers in the Victorian period were among the few who could venture into the unknown, a world in which they could move beyond a constrained female identity, becoming honorary men, able to exert control over themselves and others. Botany, collecting and painting plants were all used to justify such an escape.

As Dea Birkett shows in *Spinsters Abroad: Victorian Lady Explorers* (1991), the last border of imperial respectability was often the English gardens edging colonial buildings. Keeping the border zone neat and trim, even if the lawn and flowers were wilting in the heat, was for some women an important act of duty. For other women, entering an 'English' garden in a far-away place meant a return to an unwelcome propriety. The traveller Gertrude Bell wrote in a letter in 1892 'I shall be sorry to leave this wonderful freedom and be back within walls and gardens'; and on her travels in India, Marianne North declared from Coonoor, in 1878, that she wanted to move on 'to the dear old sun and heat again. I fancy it will suit me better than the dressy gardens and trim-shaved roads of this Anglo-Indian Paradise.'

Marianne North

The most important relationship in Marianne's life was with her father, Frederick North, a selfish, irritable and dominating man. After her mother died Marianne, then aged twenty-four, became his chaperone, housekeeper, nurse and guide and his ears (for he was deaf), both at home and on the series of European and Middle-Eastern journeys they made together.

When her father died in 1869, Marianne saw it not as an escape but as the total devastation of her world. She wrote in her diary: 'For nearly forty years he had been my one friend and companion and now I had to learn to live without him and to fill up my life with other interests as best I might.'

Two years after her father's death, she set out to travel to North and South America, the Caribbean, India, Australasia and Africa. She had wanted to travel to the tropics ever since Sir William Hooker, the Director of Kew, gave her some *Amherstia nobilis*, one of the most exotic flowers in existence. Marianne was not an independent traveller. She was always accompanied by a guide and carried letters of introduction to the local English community. Her role remained that of an observer: once, in India, and staying in a guest house at Christmas, she watched the wives of British soldiers prepare a festive dinner but stayed apart for fear that they might 'snub such a shabby old thing'.

Marianne was plagued by psychosomatic illness and if she lingered too long in one spot, became ill, developing rheumatism of the thumb and aches in her feet: the solution was always new horizons and more restless travelling.

In 1885, Marianne returned to England from a last escape – an expedition to South America. Her 'nerves' were causing trouble. (In 1884, when in quarantine in the Seychelles she had felt persecuted by strange voices.) So she rented a house in the Cotswolds, built a greenhouse for cuttings from Kew and dug up the tennis court (she had always hated the game) to make an English garden. In her autobiography (1892), she wrote:

> I found the exact place, I wished for, and already my garden is becoming
> famous among those who love plants; and I hope it may serve to keep my
> enemies, the so-called 'nerves', quiet for the few years which are left to me to
> live. The recollections of my happy life will also be a help to my old age. No
> life is as charming as a country one in England, and no flowers are sweeter or
> more lovely than the primroses, cowslips, bluebells and violets which grow in
> abundance all around me here.

When she died her gallery was finished, as was her book, *Recollections of a Happy Life* (1892). But the passion had gone. Her last paintings of the Cotswolds lack the vigour of her earlier work. As the writer Dea Birkett has intimated, Marianne was back inside the garden gate.

Seven Snowy Peaks seen from the Araucaria Forest, Chile
Marianne North
Oil on canvas
The Royal Botanic Gardens, Kew

Another woman traveller, a Mrs Robb of Liphook in Hampshire, discovered a euphorbia growing wild near Istanbul. The only receptacle available was her hat box, which contained an impressive bonnet. Mrs Robb's horticultural interests overcame her vanity and the specimen replaced the hat. The uprooted euphorbia was brought back to England where it flourished and spread, and was nicknamed 'Mrs Robb's Bonnet' in her honour. (Worried by the possibility that plants might be stolen from her garden at Liphook, Mrs Robb also put up signs saying *Beware of the Lycopodium*. Marauding youths from the nearby railway station were not to know this was the Latin name for clubmoss!)

Endings and beginnings

Despite the influx of new ideas and plants, many aspects of Victorian gardening encouraged respectability and conformity – carpet bedding, manicured lawns, restricted colour combination, prescribed conventions for flower arranging – all tended towards a constrained approach. But such conventions were beginning to be challenged and other influences, such as the Arts and Crafts movement were to offer new approaches to house and garden design, and to life-styles in general.

For women gardeners, the last decades of nineteenth-century England and the first of the twentieth were to be full of new opportunities.

Painting of Marianne North's garden
Marianne North
The Royal Botanic Gardens, Kew

This painting of Marianne North's Cotswold garden is very different to the more vibrant works she painted on her travels.

Education and Emancipation:
The Early Twentieth Century

Introduction

Novels, memoirs and old *Country Life* photographs all give us glimpses into the idyllic world of Edwardian England. We imagine scenes of tea on the terrace, tennis and croquet on the lawn, long flower-filled herbaceous borders, well-stocked walled kitchen gardens and willowy women in floppy hats. These visions convey images of a world which in many aspects lasted until the Second World War although by then, the vision was somewhat illusory.

To an extent these earlier images reflect reality. The economic conditions of the late nineteenth and early twentieth centuries meant that the upper echelons of society had large amounts of disposable wealth, and substantial sums were dedicated to the art of elegant living involving grand houses, beautiful gardens, and the rise of the country-house weekend. These were made possible by the development of the railway, the invention of the motorcar – and a seemingly unending supply of cheap labour for servants and gardeners.

For the upper-classes, country houses and their gardens, were still very much status symbols, a sure sign that one was part of the fabric of society. Being 'landed' was important, even if land, once thought to be safe, was in reality a risky investment – a truth that many landowners had discovered when hit by the agricultural depression of the 1880s. Some upper-class families found salvation in the worlds of business and finance. Landowners who had foresight and acumen sent their sons into business or married them to the daughters of rich businessmen, and thus the new rich – bankers, industrialists, financiers – found acceptance among the old aristocracy. Americans could now also buy their way into this world, trading marriage to their wealthy daughters for membership of the country-house set.

Many of the new rich, as the historian Mark Girouard has revealed, were inspired by the images of ivy-clad houses, perfect lawns and lush pastures that they found in the pages of *Country Life*, which was founded in 1897 by Edward Hudson. This magazine helped set tastes and fashions in country-house living and gardening, and unfailingly suggested that the closest thing to paradise was the life of an English country gentleman, even if it could only be lived at weekends.

In general, women's role in this world was to ensure the smooth running of the household, act as hostesses and as arbiters of taste and decorum. Only rarely were they patrons. Most houses and gardens were still created or improved by men of wealth and power. Despite the fact that legislation was gradually changing their social position (married women gained full legal control of their property in 1882), the laws of inheritance and the exclusion of upper- and middle-class women from the world of work meant that most could still exercise power only informally.

PREVIOUS PAGES
*The Great Plat, Hestercombe Gardens, Martin Charles.
Hestercombe Gardens Trust (detail)*

However, the great social hostesses of the period, such as Lady Emerald Cunard (1872–1948), Sibyl Colefax (1874–1950) and Nancy Astor, Viscountess Astor (1879–1964), did include gardening as part of their domain. From the 1880s it had become acceptable for women to actually work in gardens as well as to direct the armies of gardeners who maintained these expensive, labour-intensive pleasure grounds. Gardening, fashion, flower embroidery, flower arranging and interior design were all linked: they provided the embellishments of the country house. One dressed oneself, one's house and one's garden. And if one were at a loss as to how to succeed in these important accomplishments, friendly female advice might be obtained from one's guests such as Norah Lindsay.

The Long Garden, the Manor House, Sutton Courtenay, Oxfordshire
Country Life *Picture Library*

This photograph illustrated an article written by Norah Lindsay and published in Country Life *on 10 May 1931.*

Norah Lindsay (1876–1948)

Leaning gently on a sundial, in the midst of a daisy-clad lawn, on a pavement planted with thymes and santolinas, Norah Lindsay seems the epitome of Edwardian elegance. Her photograph, designed for readers of *Country Life*, still seems to crystallise an image of the glorious summer afternoons of Edwardian England.

Norah Lindsay was possibly the most celebrated gardening guest of the Edwardian period, charming her high society hosts and hostesses with her wit and vivacity and offering free advice on their borders and planting plans. When penury threatened she was persuaded to charge for her services, but since she failed to explain this to all her hostesses, she received some surprised looks when presenting her bill after a weekend of gardening tips. Nonetheless, her friends Emerald Cunard, Sibyl Colefax and Nancy Astor could easily afford to pay.

Norah's own garden, which stretched down to the banks of the Thames at Sutton Courtenay in Oxfordshire, was a thoroughly romantic planting. It had been given to her and her husband, a Colonel Harry Lindsay, as a wedding present, but although they had two children, the marriage was not happy, and the Colonel soon left Norah's life.

Norah's house and garden were the realisation of a highly self-conscious image, recorded in her own decidedly purple prose 'Bignonia [sic] is heavy with bud – in dry bilious branches – like desiccated beaks of birds.' She wanted the world to know about her achievements: 'Some gardens, like some people, have a charm potent to enslave and yet as intangible as dew or vapour. The gardens of the manor of Sutton Courtenay have this shining quality.' (Quoted in Deborah Kellaway (ed.), *The Illustrated Virago Book of Women Gardeners*, 1997.) More than a little fey, she believed that plants, flowers and trees chose their own positions: 'These were before you, these will live after you, so listen to their message and humbly follow in their sedate and simple footsteps.' (Quoted in Jane Brown, *Eminent Gardeners*, 1990.)

A love of Italy inspired her use of water in her garden and her desire to contrast dark and light: 'I would have been a much lesser gardener had I not worshipped at the crumbling shrines of the ancient garden gods of Florence and Rome.' (Jane Brown, *Eminent Gardeners*, 1990.) She built a circular pool with a raised rim; a square pool complete with a lead fountain in the shape of a baby; and a rill, or brick path inset with pools, planted with marsh marigolds and iris. In order to recreate the feel of Italy, she set her herbaceous plants against dark backgrounds, substituting Irish yews and junipers for dark Italian cypresses. (To our eyes her effects occasionally seem odd – the Long Garden at Sutton Courtenay contained a collection of phallic-looking clipped box pillars and domes, rising above mounds of flowering plants.)

Above all, though, Sutton Courtenay was a garden stuffed with flowers; the rich, sweet-scented profusion of blooms designed to provide a backdrop for summer afternoons. But underpinning all this seemingly artless profusion was a carefully constructed plan. Like Gertrude Jekyll's, Norah's planting schemes used a graded colour palette to create her preferred delicate shadings as the writer Jane Brown's research on Norah's gardening schemes has shown: '...rich blues, deep purples, various pinks and lemon yellows are allowed together but well away from the hot scarlets of poppies and the dark metallic golds of sunflowers and *Rudbeckias*'. Grey foliage and sculptural and architectural plants such as thistles were used to break up the borders and add interest.

The drifts of colour in her planting schemes entranced Norah's friends. Nancy Astor asked her to transform Cliveden for the Ascot house parties, so Norah packed the parterres with forget-me-nots, producing a sea of blue. Norah's advice was soon in great demand. At Blickling she swept away Lady Lothian's parterre of the 1870s, replacing it with a simplified arrangement of broad, massed herbaceous plants. She drew up planting schemes for the MP for Hythe, Philip Sassoon, at Trent Park, Middlesex, and Port Lympne in Kent, softening the grand formal terraces at Port Lympne with purple, blue, pink and mauve asters and stripes of golden yellow and glowing scarlet dahlias. Norah also influenced the famous plantsman Lawrence Johnston in his garden at Hidcote Manor in Gloucestershire, and many years later in the 1930s and 1940s, worked with him to create a seemingly haphazard abundance of flowers set against a backdrop of perfectly trimmed hedges.

The influence of Norah's gardening style has been profound. The use of pavements softened with plants, box-hedged beds, clumps of seemingly self-sown plants such as gypsophila and santolina, carefully graded colour combinations and artfully placed pots and tubs are now hallmarks of English gardening style, but all owe their initial popularity to her.

Norah Lindsay (1876–1948) in the grounds of the Manor House, Sutton Courtenay, Oxfordshire, 1903 (detail) Country Life *Picture Library*

at Henry Cole's School of Art in South Kensington. This was a bold step for a woman of her day. Practical and spirited, she associated with many of the members of the Arts and Crafts movement. She travelled in Italy, Greece and North Africa, and on her return to England, turned from the fine arts to interior decoration: silver and metalwork, embroidery and gilding. Jekyll became a skilled craftswoman, but as a 'lady' of independent means, was viewed as an amateur rather than as a professional. These were clearly accomplishments, but were they art?

In 1891, Jekyll was forced by her failing eyesight to abandon close work. She turned instead to gardening, bringing to it her painter's sense of colour and form and her craftswoman's eye for shape and texture. Her myopia, in many ways a personal disaster, was also a gift. The blurring of colour and form in the distance gave her a glowing Impressionistic sense of the overall effect of her designs. But this was combined with a sense of the structure, texture and smell of plants which came from minute observation. Gertrude Jekyll's works reveal an ardent sensualist and a lover of the natural world. However, her sensuality was moderated by restraint, a sense of the rightness of things: 'No artificial planting can ever equal that of nature, but one may learn from it the great lesson of the importance of moderation and reserve, of simplicity of intention and directness of purpose, and the inestimable value of the quality called breadth in painting.' (Gertrude Jekyll, *Wood and Garden*, 1899.)

ABOVE
Gertrude Jekyll digging a sunflower
Sir Edwin Lutyens, 6 August 1897
Dr Jane Ridley

LEFT
Gertrude Jekyll (1843–1932)
Sir William Nicholson, 1920
Oil on canvas, 762 x 762mm (30 x 30")
National Portrait Gallery, London (NPG 3334)

Lutyens had to work hard to persuade Gertrude Jekyll to sit for her portrait; she was deeply insecure about her appearance and the portrait was a brave act of self-exposure. Nicholson painted her after work, by lamplight and in front of her fire.

RIGHT
Gertrude Jekyll as an angel
Sir Edwin Lutyens, 6 August 1899
RIBA Library

The turning point in her life came in 1889, when she met the young architect Edwin Lutyens. They met at a tea party during which her awkwardness prevented her from speaking to him. However, on departing, she invited him to her house for tea, an event which marked the beginning of their friendship.

Both drew inspiration from the Surrey countryside, understanding how its vernacular architecture was almost rooted in the folds of the hills, and Munstead Wood, the house designed and built by Lutyens to fit into Jekyll's existing garden, cemented their friendship, with Lutyens creating for 'Bumps', as he called her, a work of solid but refined craftsmanship.

From there, the two of them went on to create over a hundred gardens; Lutyens's dramatic sense of form and line creating a range of spaces that Jekyll gilded and embroidered with plants and flowers. Both had a sense of detail, of the texture of brick and stone, with Jekyll adding plants to enhance form and line, and Lutyens allowing his carefully constructed stonework to be softened by pillows of plants. Together they resolved the usual tension between architect and gardener, each contributing to a harmonious whole.

Jekyll and Lutyens created gardens for many different buildings: modest cottages as well as castles, each design a carefully crafted balance of architectural form and thoughtful planting. However by the 1920s, Lutyens's life was dominated by his building of New Delhi (first commissioned in 1912), while Jekyll's physical horizons were the boundaries of Munstead Wood.

Although she became increasingly reclusive, Gertrude Jekyll was widely known. In 1899 she had published her first book, *Wood and Garden*, illustrated with her own photographs. She went on to write another fifteen books and over 1,000 articles. Her fame attracted visitors, the more privileged of whom were shown her garden, with Jekyll insisting on taking her visitors round herself, so that they could see the garden through her eyes.

Gertrude Jekyll died on 8 December 1932. Her tombstone, designed by Lutyens, has the simple inscription: *Gertrude Jekyll: Artist, Gardener, Craftswoman*. Few of her gardens survive as she designed them, but her approach to the process of gardening, her delight in the varied forms of the natural world, her sense of colour and form, all elevated gardening to the status of a fine art.

The Great Plat, Hestercombe Gardens
Martin Charles
Hestercombe Gardens Trust

Hestercombe

Hestercombe, near Taunton, is one of Edwin Lutyens's and Gertrude Jekyll's finest collaborations, a garden of both intimate and grand spaces, opening onto vistas of the Somerset hills.

The centrepiece of the garden is the Great Plat, a square sunken garden interspersed with grass paths. Stone paving delineates the beds and emphasises the pattern. The planting is carefully controlled to create an overall effect but also to reveal details of leaf and flower, as plants are contrasted against stone or brick. At one end the Plat is enclosed by a massive oak pergola, 70 metres (230') long, with alternating square and round stone pillars from which hang tangled roses, clematis and Russian vine. On each side of the Plat are two long, narrow, stone-edged rills, planted with water forget-me-nots, arums, yellow musk and iris. The plants subtly fit their setting, the perfection of the vertical waxy white arums rising from a pool punctuating the horizontal rhythm of the rill.

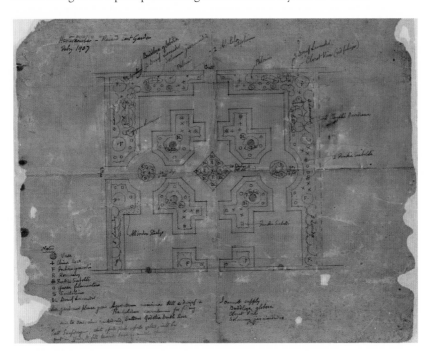

LEFT
Planting Plan for the Dutch or East Garden
Ink on paper
Somerset County Record Office

In the almost-square Dutch or East Garden Gertrude Jekyll used spiky yuccas surrounded by stachys, cat-mint and lavender. These were among her favourite plants and appeared frequently in her gardens.

RIGHT
The Dutch or East Garden, Hestercombe Gardens
Andrew Lawson
Hestercombe Gardens Trust

The Hestercombe Gardens Trust is restoring the garden to show how it looked when Edwin Lutyens and Gertrude Jekyll created it.

Gertrude Jekyll and colour

Victorian gardens had been vibrant with ribbon and carpet bedding, in bold primary colours. In the late nineteenth and early twentieth centuries new ideas on the use of colour in the garden came into vogue.

As an art student, the young Gertrude Jekyll studied J.M.W. Turner's use of colour and was influenced by the gardening journalist William Robinson's beliefs on natural colour. Jane Brown believes that Gertrude Jekyll, like the painters Claude Monet and Paul Cézanne, was also strongly influenced by the theory of colour evolved by Michel-Eugène Chevreul (1786–1889). Chevreul's theories, first published in 1839, drew upon a colour circle: an outside ring of primary colours – red, yellow and blue – with an inner ring of graduated tones and secondary colours – orange, violet and green. Harmony is achieved through the various relationships within the colour circle: adjacent colours create harmony, as do the contrasts between opposites. The use of black and white enhances shades, tints and tones. Sequences of colour can be stabilised by using a dark colour, which explains the use of yew and other dark evergreens in Jekyll's gardens. White, by contrast, is a colour of light and is used to 'bring out' other colours.

The colour scheme of the 61 metre (200') long herbaceous border at Munstead Wood reveals Jekyll's deep understanding of colour. She used plants to weave a three-dimensional Impressionist tapestry, heightened by careful contrasts which prevented harmony degenerating into monotony.

The border began softly with white flowers set amidst grey and silvery foliage – stachys, santolina, sea kale and lyme grass. These were followed by warm white, pale pink, grey-blue and pale blue flowers, and reached a central crescendo of yellow, orange, mahogany and scarlet, with tall spires of tiger lilies, hollyhocks, gladioli and dahlias. The order was then reversed and the observer taken back down through the spectrum. Throughout, colour was expertly combined. Blues were set against blues and then against purples to bring out their depth, or against contrasts of white or yellow to heighten their effect. Behind the border, the stone wall, clothed in evergreens, provided a backdrop framing the colours.

Jekyll, however, was painting with living things, and this required an encyclopaedic knowledge of plants. Moreover, the picture was not stable – plants flowered and died, and maintenance was constant hard work: staking, tying down, dead-heading and seasonal planting.

It was a transitory art, captured in Gertrude Jekyll's own photographs and in the paintings of her garden by the watercolourist Helen Allingham (see page 93), but inevitably subject to time and decay.

The red section of the south border at Munstead Wood Autochrome, c.1912
Country Life *Picture Library*

Easton Lodge

In 1902 Daisy commissioned the architect and landscape designer Harold Peto (1854–1933) to transform the main gardens at Easton Lodge into an Italianate garden, with sixty-seven inebriates from a Salvation Army home being employed for the heavy work. Despite the fact that Peto referred to it as 'a small Sat to Mon villa garden', it was one of his grandest creations. Around the old croquet lawn, Peto built arched pergolas, dripping with roses and climbing plants and forming galleries of scented greenery. Beyond lay a maze, woodland walks and a tree-house, to say nothing of a 30 metre (100') balustraded pool on which floated water lilies. Not content with this, Daisy added an exotic Japanese garden with lanterns and a teahouse. This was the ultimate garden for the golden afternoons of Edwardian England, for high-society entertaining and scandalous love affairs, yet Easton was also the scene for uplifting socialist gatherings, with Sidney and Beatrice Webb, Ramsay MacDonald and Bernard Shaw replacing the Prince of Wales and his set.

The Orchard Garden
Ellen Willmott, Warley Place photograph album (page 22), c.1910
Royal Horticultural Society, Lindley Library

Ellen Willmott was the last in a long line of wealthy gardeners at Warley Place in Essex, where her family had moved in 1876. In 1888, having inherited a fortune from her godmother, she spent much of her wealth on plants for Warley Place and on the restoration of a garden she had bought near Aix-les-Bains in France. In 1905 she bought another garden in Italy, and at one point was employing over 100 gardeners. Every year she photographed them in their smart uniforms – but was reluctant to give them good references if they tried to leave.

Famous for her ability to nurture rare species, Ellen lavished time and effort on finding the right conditions for germinating seeds. Her first love was daffodils, but she was also famous for her primula hybrids and roses, and eventually had over 100,000 varieties of plants at Warley Place. Her book *Warley Garden in Spring and Summer*, published in 1909, contains her own photographs of the drifts of daffodils and spring flowers as well as the summer borders brimming over with luscious plants. She also commissioned Alfred Parsons (1847–1920) to make the drawings for her two-volume *Genus Rosa* (1910–14; a publishing disaster).

What Ellen possessed, she also protected. In 1900 she made the Head Gardener fix up a trip wire around the daffodil fields. If an intruder broke through, a series of air guns went off. She also gained a reputation for meanness, reputedly watching her guests anxiously as they toured her gardens in case they took as much as a cutting or a seed head. She helped sponsor Ernest Wilson's plant-hunting expeditions to China at the turn of the century but named the plants she raised from the seeds he brought back after herself. Age brought mild paranoia as well as eccentricity and in the 1920s she carried a loaded revolver in her handbag in case of attack.

Ellen became famous for her proud, confrontational and authoritarian style. Her wealth, intelligence and knowledge enabled her to penetrate the bastions of the primarily male gardening world. She was the first woman to be elected to the Linnaean Society, was active on various RHS committees and at the age of seventy-five was still a member of the Floral Committee and the Lily Committee. Ellen attended RHS committee meetings with unusual specimens in her lapel and watched to see how many members of the committee were unable to recognise them. As her biographer, Audrey Le Lièvre, says 'There must have come a time when, almost without knowing it, she reached the point where she could no longer be bothered to conceal the fact that she was more knowledgeable, quick-witted, and intelligent than most of the men she knew.' She and Gertrude Jekyll were the only women recipients of the Victoria Medal of Honour when it was instituted in 1897.

Pride and arrogance were her downfall. Her investments lost their value so she took out mortgages and sold family treasures to survive. During the First World War, the army took over the estate and destroyed the rose collection. Without money to sustain it,

Beatrix Potter (1866–1943)
Delmar Banner, 1938
Oil on canvas, 749 x 622mm
(29½ x 24½")
National Portrait Gallery,
London (NPG 3635)

*Painted after her many books for
children had brought her fame and
fortune, this portrait shows
Beatrix's beloved Lake District
and her prize Herdwick sheep.*

Beatrix Potter

For Beatrix Potter, her writing and illustrating of her own books provided her first means of escape, mentally and physically, from the constraints of family life in London into a world of her own. A determined and independent young girl, she struggled with the tension between her strong will and her innate shyness and introversion. Her temperament, coupled with her parents' cautious and restrictive vision of the world, was a barrier to her own fulfilment.

For the millions of adults who grew up on her books, Beatrix Potter's gardens have become the archetypal cottage garden, an idyll of childhood. But Mr McGregor's garden, with its paved walks, lily pond and beds of soporific lettuces, was a place of dangerous adventure – one could, after all, end up as a pie.

Beatrix had fallen in love with the scenery and wildlife of the Lake District while on holiday with her parents. (Mr McGregor's vegetable garden and wicket gate were based on the garden of Lingholm, near Keswick.) The royalties from her books eventually enabled her, in 1905, to buy Hill Top Farm at Sawrey, a small village between Coniston and Windermere. The garden at Hill Top appears in several of her books, particularly in *The Tale of Tom Kitten* (1907). In a letter of July 1924, Beatrix described it as a regular old-fashioned farm garden:

> …with a box hedge round the flower bed, and moss roses and pansies and
> black currants & strawberries and peas – and big sage bushes for Jemima, but
> onions always do badly. I have tall white bell flowers I am fond of, they are just
> going over, next there will be phlox; and last come the michaelmas daisies and
> chrysanthemums. Then soon after Christmas we have snowdrops, they grow
> wild and come up all over the garden & orchard, and some in the woods.
> (Extract from *Beatrix Potter's Letters*, selected by Judy Taylor, 1989)

Here she fulfilled her ambition to be a Lake District farmer, and here, after wringing agreement from her parents, in 1913 she married Willie Heelis, her solicitor. Paradise had the odd wickedness, however – she once said that all the flowers in her garden had been given to her, apart from honesty, which she stole.

With her Arcadia achieved, Beatrix wrote less and less. Her eyesight was failing, and she concentrated instead on breeding the Herdwick sheep that appear in her portrait (opposite). On her death, she left her farm and land to the National Trust, her generous donation protecting her Arcadia for others.

Dreams and Diversity:
The Twentieth Century to the Present Day

to return there. Her bisexuality may also be linked to her intense, frustrated longing for the place. Had she been a man it would have been her inheritance. Certainly, both Knole and her sexual orientation lie behind Virginia Woolf's portrayal of Vita as Orlando in the book of the same name, and they may, in part, provide a key to Sissinghurst, the garden that she and her husband Harold Nicolson created.

In 1930, when she discovered Sissinghurst, it was a ruined and neglected sixteenth-century castle, set in a sea of rubbish. Vita described it thus: 'Some high Tudor walls of pinkish brick remained as the anatomy of the garden-to-be, and two stretches of a much older moat provided a black mirror of quiet water in the distance.' (Quoted in Dawn MacLeod, *Down-to-Earth Women*, 1982.) She fell instantly in love. It was Sleeping Beauty's castle and she was the prince who could bring it to life. Moreover, it had good soil and ancestral links with Knole. There were no doubts.

The garden at Sissinghurst combined Harold's love of classical symmetry with Vita's romantic excess; an indissoluble bond between them in a sometimes difficult marriage. Moreover the garden allowed Vita the space she needed in which to be herself. Fiercely independent, she felt a strong desire to control but hated any sense of being controlled herself. She believed she had to struggle for recognition more than a man. The garden was her refuge, her escape. The place was, as Harold realised, 'a succession of privacies: the forecourt, the first arch, the main court, the tower arch, the lawn, the orchard. All a series of escapes from the world, giving the impression of cumulative escape.'

Vita had hated the fact that Knole had passed into the care of the National Trust, and her fury when it was suggested ten years before her death that Sissinghurst should go to the Trust was intense.

> Never, never, never. Au grand jamais, jamais. Never, never, never. Not that hard
> little metal plaque at my door, Nigel can do what he likes when I am dead, but
> as long as I live no Nat. Trust or any other foreign body shall have my darling.
> No, no. Over my corpse or my ashes; not otherwise. It is bad enough to have
> lost my Knole, but they shan't take Sissinghurst from me ... They shan't; they
> shan't; I won't; they can't make me. I won't, they can't make me, I never would...
>
> (Quoted in Jane Brown, *Sissinghurst: Portrait of a Garden*, 1998)

But after her death her son Nigel found a note saying she would understand if he did.

Sissinghurst was, in part, Vita's replacement for Knole. The garden draws some of its inspiration from the secretive spaces of Knole: courtyards, rooms, corridors, private spaces. But in creating her own most private, inner space, she transcended Knole and spoke to the thousands of visitors whose sensitivities are still awakened by her intimate vision.

Sissinghurst: the creation of a garden

For two years, Vita and Harold cleared out rubbish: old bedsteads, bottles and tins, the debris of neglect. Harold discovered his architectural talents, spending hours with measuring tapes and squared paper, trying to camouflage the site's basic lack of symmetry. His design set down axial walks to the four points of the compass, each defined by hedges of hornbeam or yew and culminating in a terminal point such as a statue or archway. More intimate rooms opened off the walks, 'rather as the rooms of an enormous house would open off the arterial corridors,' Vita wrote (*RHS Journal*, 1953). (Courtyards, rooms, corridors – all of course echoed Knole.)

Once this framework was in place, they began planting lavishly, agreeing on a mix of tall, elegant plants – delphiniums, eremurus, verbascums and iris – and carpets of smaller plants. (The only plant they disagreed about was the red-hot poker, which she significantly adored and he loathed.) Vita hung the castle walls with honeysuckles and clematis and set rambling roses to entwine themselves through the apple trees in the orchard (she loved the perfection of immaculately trimmed hedges but would let plants flop in profusion), while Harold underplanted the lime walk with spring flowers.

The White Garden, perhaps the most famous garden in England, was begun in the winter of 1949. Vita's garden really contained grey, green and white flowers and foliage. But the use of white, with its echo of purity and chastity, created the predominant effect and this was reinforced by the placing of a statue of the Virgin within the enclosure. Vita's garden combines formality and informality: one area a pattern of box-edged rectangles, planted with single varieties of white flowers; the other containing regal lilies, the flowers of the Annunciation, which soar upwards from beds of silver and grey foliage. The centrepiece is an arbour, a canopy of white roses, cascading to the floor in a flurry of petals.

Sissinghurst's White Garden was created in the public eye. Vita charted its progress in her *Observer* column, which she wrote for nearly fifteen years until 1961. Her style was practical, simple and personal, with just the right amount of romance. She liked talking about lindens, garths or rondels, and nut-plats, rather than lime trees, lawns and nut walks. Vita also opened her garden to visitors, the 'shillingses' as she called them. The popularity of the place has not waned since then.

Part of the garden at Sissinghurst Castle with a view of the Tower, as it was during Vita's lifetime
Country Life *Picture Library*

Looking across the White Garden at Sissinghurst to the Towers of the Castle, with the Rosa Longicuspis *covered canopy and arum lilies in the foreground*
The National Trust

Establishing identities — the changing role of women

The role and position of women changed dramatically in the twentieth century. In 1900 women could not vote, their access to education and employment was restricted and they were still largely confined to a domestic world. By the end of the century, women's rights to education and employment opportunities were taken for granted. The twentieth century also allowed women access to a more diverse range of identities than those of daughter, wife and mother. For some women, gardens were retreats, places of contemplation and introspection; for others, practical activity was a springboard to a successful career in the commercial gardening world.

Transforming lives

Even flower arranging, for a time a despised art, has been for many women a route to new interests and self-fulfilment. This was the case for Constance Spry (1886–1960). Constance had always wanted to be a gardener but her father did not think it a suitable career. So she went to Ireland, where she became a lecturer and contracted a disastrous marriage. Escaping from this, she settled down in Abinger in Surrey with H.E. Spry. Here she was at last able to indulge her passion for gardens and flowers. She soon gained a reputation, first by sending displays of flowers from her home in Surrey to smart London shops. Her eye-catching arrangements were so successful that she was able to open her own shop, first in Pimlico, then in fashionable South Audley Street, and in 1946, she started a school at Winkfield Place.

Constance's clients came from high society: she did the flowers for the wedding of Queen Elizabeth II and Prince Philip as well as for the Coronation, but her ideas spread further, with classes on flower arranging becoming a staple item at gardening clubs and Women's Institutes. For many women in the 1950s, these classes offered opportunities to meet new friends and widen limited horizons.

For many women, gardening also provided an opportunity to enrich the later part of their lives, taken up as an interest when their children had left home, lawns were no longer a requirement and borders safe from footballs. Margery Fish was a latecomer to gardening.

Valerie Finnis (b.1925)

Valerie Finnis is a product of the Waterperry School of gardening. It was here that she learned to get her hands dirty and to relish the sheer physicality of gardening. It was a love that has lasted a lifetime. 'I love digging, with my thirty-year-old stainless steel spade (perhaps it is even older than that, I cannot quite remember). It warms me up when I have a cold job to do, like tying climbers to the walls.' (Quoted in Deborah Kellaway (ed.), *The Illustrated Virago Book of Women Gardeners*, 1997.)

During the war Valerie maintained a 25-acre field of vegetables and drove trucks of fruit to Covent Garden in the early morning light. After the war she joined Waterperry as a member of staff and started to grow alpines. She built up a nursery, exchanging plants with everyone who was anyone in gardening, including Nancy Lindsay, Norah's daughter, and Margery Fish.

Valerie worked at Waterperry for twenty-eight years until her marriage to Sir David Scott, a famous plant collector. Marriage meant she had to move her vast collection of alpines to their home at the Dower House, Boughton, in Northamptonshire. Sir David looked

Valerie Finnis (b.1925)
Jan Baldwin, 1993
Colour photograph
Jan Baldwin

after his collection of rare shrubs and trees while Valerie nurtured her alpines and grew fruit and vegetables. They grew plants for open days under the National Gardens Scheme and welcomed the hordes who came to visit. She also became an accomplished photographer.

After her husband died, Valerie dispersed some of her alpine collection, but continued to garden (she once said she couldn't ever be away from her plants for more than two days). For her, plants and gardening have been a route to friendships and a rich and happy life.

Margery Fish (1892–1969)

Margery Fish worked for the *Daily Mail* as secretary and personal assistant to the editor, marrying her employer, Walter Fish, when she was almost fifty. In 1937, worried by the threat of war, the Fishes bought East Lambrook Manor in Somerset, comprising a dilapidated house and a neglected garden. Here Walter taught Margery about gardening.

Although some of his instructions were sound, other

elements displayed mere prejudice. He rightly insisted that form and structure were essential to a garden, but at times Walter must have made Margery's live difficult; he suffocated her plants with dollops of manure and over-watered her finely worked soil so that it turned into densely packed, impermeable clay. On one occasion, he insisted that she insert poles for roses in beds she had carefully prepared to be a tapestry of low-growing plants.

Margery's intuitive good taste and understanding of plants was overwhelmed by Walter's flashy approach to planting. He was essentially 'a dahlia, delphinium and lupin man' (Helen Penn, *An Englishwoman's Garden*, 1993). The dahlias in particular were obsessively worshipped, planted on 1 May and lifted on 1 November, both Stock Exchange holidays. The tubers were a job-lot and, as there were no labels, there could be no planting plan. Walter nonetheless insisted they were inserted in Margery's flower border, their vibrant colours destroying her gentle combinations of muted tones.

Although Margery was shattered by Walter's death, it opened new doors. She dug up some of the concrete between the paving slabs of Walter's paths and planted creeping plants, thymes, sunroses, alyssum, *Dianthus carthusianorum var. multiflorus*, and cheiranthus. Plants were allowed to spill over onto lawns and paths as well as being embedded into cracks in the walls. Margery hated bare earth and her borders combined shrubs, bulbs, foliage plants and annuals. She pursued weeds with fervour and believed that tracing bindweed, that 'tenacious

Margery Fish (1892–1969)
Valerie Finnis
Colour print, 305 x 254mm (12 x 10")
Royal Horticultural Society, Lindley Library

Judas of a weed' was one of the greatest pleasures in life, only surpassed by making a bonfire of the roots. But she loved ground-cover plants: bugle, prunella, stachys, lamiums, periwinkles and violets were all favourites.

Margery and her friends were keen collectors of plants. She quizzed old ladies in their cottage gardens and raided derelict sites. She wrote several books, and radio broadcasts and lectures followed. She was an enthralling performer, illustrating her talks with plant specimens, which she would then offer for sale. She grew cuttings and germinated seeds on her window ledge and then, as demand increased, started a nursery. The secretary had become a celebrity.

East Lambrook Manor Garden
South Somerset District Council Tourism and Cultural Services Unit

Work and war

The First World War had created many opportunities for women. The Second World War did the same. The historian Sue Bruley has suggested that over 80,000 women responded to the call to 'Lend a hand on the land.' Although government propaganda campaigns suggested that the work was pleasant, and depicted land girls as rosy-cheeked and smiling, stacking bales of corn under the summer sun, this was often a far cry from reality. The work was hard, living conditions austere and women were never paid at the same rate as men. Nevertheless, they helped to double Britain's food production during the war.

The *Dig for Victory* campaign allowed considerable numbers of women to contribute to the war effort. Women were encouraged to stop growing flowers and turn their gardens

Dig for Victory
Unknown photographer, August 1942
Imperial War Museum (HU36120)

In April 1941, local residents were allowed to start allotments in Kensington Gardens under the shadow of the Albert Memorial. By August 1942, when this photograph was taken, they had turned the land into productive vegetable plots.

over to vegetables instead. Those with large gardens were exhorted to keep chickens and even a pig. Municipal parks were turned into allotment gardens for those families without any land. Even the moat at the Tower of London was used to grow vegetables. The Ministry of Food under Lord Woolton sent out a constant stream of propaganda and cooks such as Marguerite Patten gave advice about preparing and eating home-grown vegetables.

Hedgerows were another source of food. When the Ministry of Health began a systematic research into the drug value of native and cultivated herbs, the National Federation of Women's Institutes was asked to help. Elderflower cordial, rosehip syrup, hedgerow jam, nettle soup, dandelion coffee and mint tea all appeared in recipe books.

The natural and vulnerable world

A thread of interest in herbalism and organic gardening has run alongside the scientific developments of the twentieth century. Women have played a key role in this. The first Culpeper herb shop was opened by Hilda Leyel in 1927. This was a return to the past, since herbalism, once an area of serious study, had languished for over a century. The shop was such a success that Hilda was able to develop as a consultant herbalist. In 1936, the Society of Herbalists was inaugurated as a result of her work.

Eleanour Sinclair Rohde (1881–1950) studied history at Oxford but like other women of her generation, was not allowed to take her degree. However, her research into medieval gardens was the source of her interest in herbs. Shy, solitary and slightly mystical, she divided her time between the British Museum Library and her garden, writing imaginative recreations of historic gardens in her books, which she then filled with descriptions of famous figures from the past. But Eleanour could be practical as well as fey. Her contribution to the war effort included *The War-time Vegetable Book* – a natural topic for an ardent vegetarian.

Women have also been involved in the conservation movement, which has taken shape from a number of sources. One such is the Soil Association, with its combination of mystical faith in muck and the practical scientific study of micro-organisms. An early pioneer was Lady Eve Balfour (1898–1990), who wrote *The Living Soil* (1943), which identified the importance of micro-organisms and humus. In 1946, the Soil Association was registered. Its approach, according to Lady Eve, was holistic.

It came to stand among its growing membership for an attitude to Life itself. The attitude is usually described as the ecological approach or the philosophy of wholeness – the logical outcome of the positive approach ... Those who believe in wholeness know that we can increase our knowledge only by admitting ignorance, cultivating humility, enlarging our field of vision through learning to see ecologically, by respecting life – not wantonly destroying it.

(Quoted in Dawn MacLeod, *Down-to-Earth Women*, 1982)

Following the inauguration of the society, Lady Eve experimented with conservation methods on her farm in Suffolk and embarked on a series of fact-finding and lecture tours in America, Australia and New Zealand. Gradually the importance of long-term conservation became accepted and organically grown wholefood became more widely available.

Queen Anne's Lace
The Gardens at Ashton Wold
Photograph by Dame Miriam Rothschild

Miriam Rothschild (b.1908)

Miriam Rothschild is a champion of ecology and conservation. She belongs to a long line of amateur enthusiasts whose professional approach to their work has merited huge respect. A naturalist, eminent scientist and Fellow of the Royal Society, she has also been described as the 'Queen of the Fleas' (because of her research into them). Miriam espoused the cause of wild flower gardening and conservation long before it became fashionable, and has enabled many people to see the value of native species and thus transform a sea of weeds into a wild flower meadow.

A granddaughter of the influential and wealthy banker Nathaniel Rothschild, Miriam spent some of her childhood at his house at Tring in Hertfordshire. Her father was a naturalist and collector, and her uncle Walter Rothschild, the 2nd Lord Rothschild, was a world-famous zoologist who published more than 800 papers and built up vast natural history collections. (He also trained a team of zebras to pull a carriage — an amazing feat as they are reputedly impossible to train.)

Miriam inherited her father's estate, Ashton Wold, from her mother in 1940. The family home came complete with eight gardeners, herbaceous and rose borders, a walled kitchen garden, glasshouses and water gardens, but like many such gardens it gradually decayed during the war years, while Miriam was working in a scientific laboratory and decoding at Bletchley. The borders were abandoned and the alpines and water garden became overgrown.

In 1970, when she was in her sixties, Miriam returned to live at Ashton Wold. The house had already been reduced in size, transformed from a baronial hall into a manor house, and was now encased in foliage. Around the walls, Miriam planted a mixture of wild and cultivated climbers: ivies, virginia creeper, wild roses and ramblers, honeysuckle and laburnum, plus quince and a white buddleia. Appalled by the declining number of wild flowers, she allowed the grass on three-quarters of an acre of tennis court to grow, and scattered over it wild flower seeds gathered from a nearby derelict airfield. The soil was ideal, poor and stony, and with a chalky element. Although she had been warned that it would take a millennium to create a medieval meadow, Miriam succeeded in producing a good imitation in just ten years. Gradually the number of species increased. After ten years, wild orchids appeared and after fifteen, there were almost 100 species of flowering plants and grasses.

Miriam's work has influenced many organisations and people. The National Trust has adopted some of her ideas, and the Prince of Wales has worked with her to create a wild flower garden at Highgrove in Gloucestershire. She was awarded the Victorian Medal of Honour by the Royal Horticultural Society for wild flower cultivation. The Ashton Wold project produces wild flower mixes for road verges, unmown areas of large gardens and waste ground. Thanks to Miriam, meadows full of moon daisies, vibrant scarlet poppies, mayweed, cornflowers and corn cockle are no longer found only in the pages of the nineteenth-century novel but are real possibilities. Miriam's 'Farmers' Nightmare' seed mix has fought back.

Dame Miriam Rothschild (b.1908)
Nick Sinclair, 1993
Bromide print, 318 x 318mm
(12½ x 12½")
National Portrait Gallery, London
(NPG P564(20))

Diversity

Gardening is now one of the nation's favourite pastimes. The development of so-called 'new towns' in the 1950s resulted in the provision of millions of small front and back gardens, each illustrating its owner's individuality. The English love of small private gardens is apparent from the skies above Heathrow, the pattern of small plots a unique patchwork of possession.

Rosemary Verey (b.1918)

Rosemary Verey, like Margery Fish, was a comparative latecomer to gardening but has become a highly influential garden designer and writer. A graduate in social history, she is interested in the history of garden design and collects early gardening books.

Her garden evolved outwards from her house (built in 1697) at Barnsley in Gloucestershire. Her starting point was the stone path outside her drawing-room door. She softened its hardness by sowing rockroses, then created a lime walk (*Tilia platyphyllos rubra*) and a laburnum avenue underplanted with alliums. Over the years she has added new features, each contributing a new identity to the garden. Her style, like those of many other twentieth-century gardeners, is informal within a formal framework.

Rosemary Verey's work has been featured in *Country Life, Vogue, House and Garden* and in Sunday colour supplements. Her book *The Englishwoman's Garden* (1980), has become a classic of its type. She has also advised her neighbour, Prince Charles, on his gardening projects at Highgrove, and created a garden for Elton John. One of her most influential innovations, or rather rediscoveries, was the ornamental potager. Inspired by her box-edged plots of ornamental lettuces, pink and yellow cabbages, ruby chard, arbours of vines and runner beans, many other gardeners have followed her example. She lectures frequently in the USA.

Barnsley House, Gloucestershire
Photograph by Andrew Lawson
Rosemary Verey

Rosemary Verey (b.1918)
Howard Sooley, 10 June 1996
C-type colour print, 373 x 294mm
(14¾ x 11½")
National Portrait Gallery, London (x88507)

This photograph of Rosemary Verey was taken in her
famous laburnum avenue, one of the major features
of her garden at Barnsley House.

Margaret Fuller (b.1936)

Margaret Fuller moved to Crossing House, Shepreth, in Cambridgeshire in 1959. She found her new garden bounded by a busy road and the King's Cross to Cambridge railway line. She and her husband rapidly set to work to hide the dismal surroundings. Money was in short supply so they had to improvise. Margaret decided the garden lacked character and height, so she persuaded her husband to build raised alpine beds, using old railway uniforms dug into the soil to add drainage. The beds, planted with alpines and bulbs, delight passers-by, especially those on the trains. Short of space, the Fullers gardened right up to the rails, and even created a vegetable plot 500 yards up the line. Resourceful, determined and passionate, Margaret shows how visions can take shape despite adversity. Her original style has brought delight not only to her numerous friends and visitors but also to numberless travellers.

The professional world

In the second half of the twentieth century, gardening on a large scale moved from the houses of the aristocracy to the public, urban landscape. Sylvia Crowe (1901–97), defined the principles of good garden design 'as unity, scale, time, space, division, light and shade, texture, tone and colour and styles.' She put these into practice in her projects, including work for the Forestry Commission, landscaping at Harlow and Basildon new towns and creating the entrance to the Commonwealth Institute in Kensington. When she started there was no training available in landscape design so she took a horticultural course at Swanley Horticultural College and then became a pupil in a landscape design office.

Brenda Colvin (1897–1981), also a graduate of Swanley Horticultural College, was one of the founders of the Institute of Landscape Architects and supported the landscaping of power stations, reservoirs and other sites. In her designs, plants are used as architectural shapes rather than decorative embellishments.

But despite the high quality of many of the graduates from women's gardening schools, it took time for women to penetrate the higher echelons of the world of professional gardeners. Sissinghurst is unusual in that it has had a tradition of female head gardeners from the 1950s. Now, at the turn of the millennium, women outnumber men on horticultural courses and women gardeners are managers of estates and parks. Men, however, still dominate some aspects of the profession. Women form a small minority amongst National Trust head gardeners. The first woman was only appointed to the Council of the Royal Horticultural Society (founded in 1804 – as the Horticultural Society of London) in 1968. Thus many of the most influential women gardeners continue to be self-taught, learning by doing, reading, talking to other gardeners and visiting their gardens.

Television has helped bring gardening alive for many people. Most of the early presenters were men, but the latest in the line of television horticultural personalities is Charlie Dimmock, co-presenter of the BBC's *Ground Force*. According to a recent article in the *Independent*, she is 'the horticultural world's only sex symbol.' Charlie's true significance, however, may lie more in the fact that she worked her way up through horticultural college and was employed in a garden centre before working for the BBC.

Beth Chatto is another woman who has triumphed through hard work. She is a plantswoman interested above all in the relationship of plants to their environment, particularly difficult ones. Since her home has always been in the dry, desiccated, wind-swept flat lands of Essex, she has had to learn how to transform that desert into a rich oasis of plants.

Beatrix Havergal (1901–80) with Pamela Schwerdt and Sibylle Kreutzberger
Valerie Finnis, 1960s
Colour photograph, 305 x 254mm (12 x 10")
Royal Horticultural Society, Lindley Library

Pamela Schwerdt and Sibylle Kreutzberger were graduates of the Waterperry School who later worked at Sissinghurst, overseeing its transfer to the National Trust.

Beth Chatto (b.1923)

For thirty-five years Beth Chatto was a friend of Sir Cedric Morris (1889–1982), painter and plantsman, and a group of Essex painters and gardeners which included John Nash (1893–1977) and Constance Spry. Inspired by Sir Cedric's legendary collection of species plants and bulbs, and by her husband, Andrew Chatto's lifelong study of the homes of garden plants, she learnt to deal with problem areas, finding plants adapted by nature to a wide range of conditions.

> The garden has for many people become far more than an attractive addition to the home. It is a form of therapy. The dedication and devotion needed, and the response from plants, provides both solace and inspiration, supportive through many crises that inevitably come in the course of life.
>
> (Beth Chatto quoted in Helen Penn,
> *An Englishwoman's Garden*, 1993)

In 1960, the Chattos built a new home on their fruit farm at Elmstead Market, near Colchester. The site was a wasteland, 'a confused tangle of willow, blackthorn and bramble' situated in a shallow hollow between two farms. Its hidden potential was the varying soil conditions. 'It consisted of a long spring-fed hollow where the soils lay black and waterlogged, surrounded by sun-baked gravel.' (Beth Chatto and Christopher Lloyd, *Dear Friend and Gardener*, 1998.) They contrived to convert these problem areas into advantages, eventually making a Mediterranean Garden on the gravel soil, a Woodland Garden beneath ancient oaks, and a Bog Garden in the wet hollow.

Overall, the soil was impoverished. Deep digging and drainage ditches were needed for aeration, while large compost heaps are still made and spread when and where required. Plants are grouped according to height and spread, forming roughly asymmetrical triangles rather than in serried ranks.

In 1967, Beth opened her nursery for unusual plants. She has exhibited at the Chelsea Flower Show, her stands famous for their exquisite display. Her books *The Dry Garden* (1978) and *The Damp Garden* (1982) have shed new light on the art of gardening and attracted thousands of visitors to her gardens. Her letters on life and gardening to Christopher Lloyd, published as *Dear Friend and Gardener* (1998), reveal her understanding of plants, warm humanity and delight in life, and her watchwords of balance, repetition, harmony and simplicity.

LEFT
Beth Chatto (b.1923) at the Beth Chatto Gardens, Elmstead Market, Essex
Charles Hopkinson, September 1997
Bromide print, 280 x 280mm (11 x 11")
National Portrait Gallery, London (NPG x88416)

RIGHT
Part of the Gravel Garden at the Beth Chatto Gardens, Elmstead Market, Essex
Marianne Majerus, Country Life, 25 May 1993
Marianne Majerus/Country Life Picture Library

Picture Credits

Illustrations:

Frontispiece: Photograph courtesy of the Imperial War Museum, London © Reserved; pages 1 & 91: © Reserved; pages 11 & 60: © By permission of The British Library, London; page 13 © National Gallery, London; pages 18 & 24: © National Trust Photographic Library/John Hammond; page 22: © National Trust Photographic Library/Nick Meers; page 26: © By kind permission of the Marquess of Tavistock and the Trustees of the Bedford Estate; pages 26 & 117: © RIBA Library; page 30: © National Trust Photographic Library/Stephen Robson; pages 32 & 33: © V & A Picture Library; page 36: © The Duke of Beaufort. Reproduced from *The Duchess of Beaufort's Flowers*, Webb & Bower, 1983; page 37: The Metropolitan Museum of Art, bequest of Jacob Ruppert, 1939 (39.65.3). Photograph © 1998 The Metropolitan Museum of Art; page 40: The Royal Collection © 2000, Her Majesty Queen Elizabeth II; page 43: © The Royal Borough of Kensington and Chelsea Libraries and Arts Service; page 47: © National Trust

Photographic Library/Andrew Butler; pages 48, 66 & 68: © The British Museum, London; pages 50, 51, 52, 58, 76, 80, 101, 102, 104, 106 & 129: © The Board of Trustees of the Royal Botanic Gardens, Kew; page 54: © National Trust Photographic Library/Jerry Harpur; pages 62 & 63: © Tim Imrie Tait/*Country Life* Picture Library; page 70: © National Trust Photographic Library/Vera Collingwood; page 71: © Guildhall Library, Corporation of London; page 77: Crown copyright: Historic Royal Palaces. Reproduced by permission of Historic Royal Palaces under licence from the Controller of Her Majesty's Stationery Office; page 79: © Royal Academy of Arts, London; page 83: Courtesy of the Museum of Garden History; page 84: © Sue Bennett; pages 87, 88, 111, 113, 123, 132, 133, 135 & 150: *Country Life* Picture Library; pages 89 & 136: © Royal Horticultural Society, Lindley Library; page 92: © Birmingham Museums & Art Gallery; pages 94 & 98: © Reserved; pages 108 & 118: Courtesy of the Hestercombe Gardens Trust © Martin Charles; page 115: Reproduced by permission of Elizabeth Banks © Tate, London 2000; page 117 (top): © Dr Jane Ridley; page 120: Courtesy of the Hestercombe Gardens Trust © Somerset County Council; page 121: Courtesy of the Hestercombe Gardens Trust © Andrew Lawson; page 125: © Reproduced by courtesy of The Francis Frith Collection; page 131: © Lallie Charles Cowell; page 142: National Trust Photographic Library/Peter Baistow; page 143: Copyright © Frederick Warne & Co., 1907, 1987. Reproduced

with kind permission of Frederick Warne & Co.; pages 144, 148 & 151: © National Trust Photographic Library/Andrew Lawson; page 147: © Courtesy Sotheby's, London; page 153: © Jan Baldwin; pages 154 & 169: Courtesy of Henry Boyd-Carpenter and the Royal Horticultural Society, Lindley Library © Valerie Finnis; page 155: © South Somerset District Council Tourism and Cultural Services Unit; pages 156 & 157: Photographs courtesy of the Imperial War Museum, London; page 159: © Dame Miriam Rothschild; page 161: © Nick Sinclair; page 162: Courtesy of Rosemary Verey © Andrew Lawson; page 163: © Howard Sooley; page 165: Courtesy of the Royal Horticultural Society, Lindley Library © Valerie Finnis; page 166: © Charles Hopkinson; page 167: © Marianne Majerus/*Country Life* Picture Library.

Text:

Page 143: Extract from *Beatrix Potter's Letters* selected by Judy Taylor. Copyright © Frederick Warne & Co., 1989. Reproduced with kind permission of Frederick Warne & Co.; page 100: Extract from a letter from Marianne North to Arthur Burnell taken from the volume *Marianne North. Letters to Dr Burnell 1878* © The Board of Trustees of the Royal Botanic Gardens, Kew; page 103: Extract from a letter from Marianne North to Sir Joseph Hooker taken from the volume *Kew. North Gallery 1879–1876* © The Board of Trustees of the Royal Botanic Gardens, Kew.

Index